PEARSON
Math
Makes Sense

3

Author Team

Ray Appel

Dorothy Galvin

Sharon Jeroski

Wendy Weight

Ricki Wortzman

Trevor Brown

Lorelei Gibeau

Peggy Morrow

Mignonne Wood

With Contributions from

Ralph Connelly

Angie Harding

Michael Davis

Don Jones

Steve Thomas

Sue Gordon

Jeananne Thomas

PEARSON

Publisher
Mike Czukar

Research and Communications Manager
Barbara Vogt

Publishing Team
Claire Burnett
Enid Haley
Jon Maxfield
Nirmala Nutakki
Sarah Mawson
Lynne Gulliver
David Liu
Lynda Cowan
Ruth Peckover
Cheri Westra
Jane Schell
Karen Alley
Judy Wilson

Photo Research
Heather L. Jackson

Design and Art Direction
Word & Image Design Studio Inc.

Composition
Integra Software Services Pvt. Ltd.
Lapiz Digital Services, India

PEARSON

The information and activities presented in this book have been carefully edited and reviewed. However, the publisher shall not be liable for any damages resulting, in whole or in part, from the reader's use of this material.

Brand names that appear in photographs of products in this textbook are intended to provide students with a sense of the real-world applications of mathematics and are in no way intended to endorse specific products.

The publisher wishes to thank the staff and students of Greenway School, Roberta Bondar Public School, and Wilkinson Public School for their assistance with photography.

ISBN-13   978-0-321-46935-9
ISBN-10   0-321-46935-6

Printed and bound in the United States.

 2 3 4 5 CC 13 12 11 10 09

Consultants, Advisers, and Reviewers

Series Consultants

Trevor Brown
Maggie Martin Connell
Craig Featherstone
John A. Van de Walle
Mignonne Wood

Assessment Consultant
Sharon Jeroski

Aboriginal Content Consultant
Pamela Courchene
Manitoba First Nations Education Resource Centre

Advisers and Reviewers

Pearson Education thanks its Advisers and Reviewers, who helped shape the vision for *Pearson Mathematics Makes Sense* through discussions and reviews of prototype materials and manuscript.

Alberta

Joanne Adomeit
Calgary Board of Education

Bob Berglind
Calgary Board of Education

Jacquie Bouck
Lloydminster Public School Division 99

Auriana Burns
Edmonton Public School Board

Daryl Chichak
Edmonton Catholic School District

Lissa D'Amour
Medicine Hat School District 76

Florence Glanfield
University of Alberta

Paige Guidolin
Edmonton School District 7

Jodi Mackie
Edmonton Public School Board

Laura L. Massie
Calgary R.C.S.S.D. 1

Jeffrey Tang
Calgary R.C.S.S.D. 1

British Columbia

Sandra Ball
School District 36 (Surrey)

Lorraine Baron
School District 23 (Central Okanagan)

Donna Beaumont
School District 41 (Burnaby)

Jennifer Ewart
School District 83 (North Okanagan-Shuswap)

Lori Fehr
School District 8 (Kootenay Lake)

Denise Flick
School District 20 (Kootenay-Columbia)

Marc Garneau
School District 36 (Surrey)

Linda Judd
School District 23 (Central Okanagan)

Debbie Korn
School District 20 (Kootenay-Columbia)

Selina Millar
School District 36 (Surrey)

Sandy Sheppard
School District 39 (Vancouver)

Chris Van Bergeyk
School District 23 (Central Okanagan)

Denise Vuignier
School District 41 (Burnaby)

Sheri Webster
School District 83 (North Okanagan-Shuswap)

Mignonne Wood
Formerly School District 41 (Burnaby)

Manitoba

Heather Anderson
Louis Riel School Division

Rosanne Ashley
Winnipeg School Division

Joanne Barré
Louis Riel School Division

Ralph Mason
University of Manitoba

Christine Ottawa
Mathematics Consultant, Winnipeg

Jean Anne Overand
Fort La Bosse School District

Gretha Pallen
Formerly Manitoba Education

Brenda Scoular
Winnipeg School Division

Pat Steuart
St. James-Assiniboia School Division

Gay Sul
Frontier School Division

Saskatchewan

Susan Beaudin
File Hills Qu'Appelle Tribal Council

Dr. Edward Doolittle
First Nations University, University of Regina

Betina Fisher
Holy Trinity Catholic School Division

Lori Jane Hantelmann
Regina School Division 4

Angie Harding
Regina R.C.S.S.D. 81

Deb Karakochuk
Greater Saskatoon Catholic Schools

Lori Saigeon
Regina Public School Board

Cheryl Shields
Spirit School Division

Heather Taylor-Berriault
Regina Public School Board

Heather Thomas
Regina Public School Board

Table of Contents

UNIT 7 Data Analysis

UNIT 8 Multiplication and Division

Welcome to

Pearson Math Makes Sense 3

Math helps you understand what you see and do every day.

You will use this book to learn about the math around you. Here's how.

In each Unit:

- A scene from the world around you reminds you of some of the math you already know.

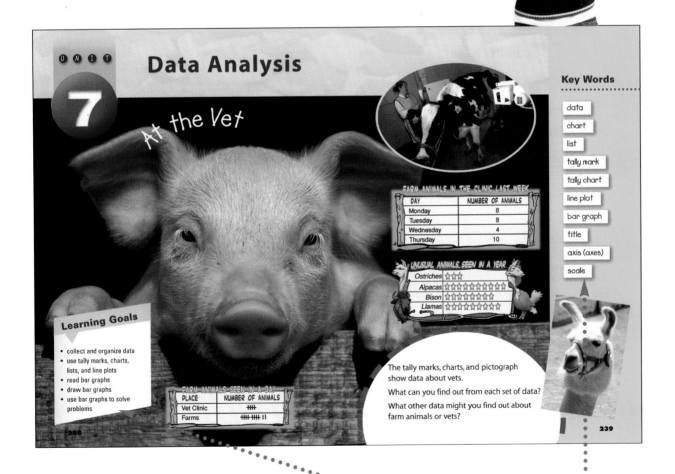

Find out what you will learn in the **Learning Goals**. Check the **Key Words**.

In each Lesson:

You **Explore** an idea or problem, usually with a partner. You often use materials.

Then you **Show and Share** your results with other students.

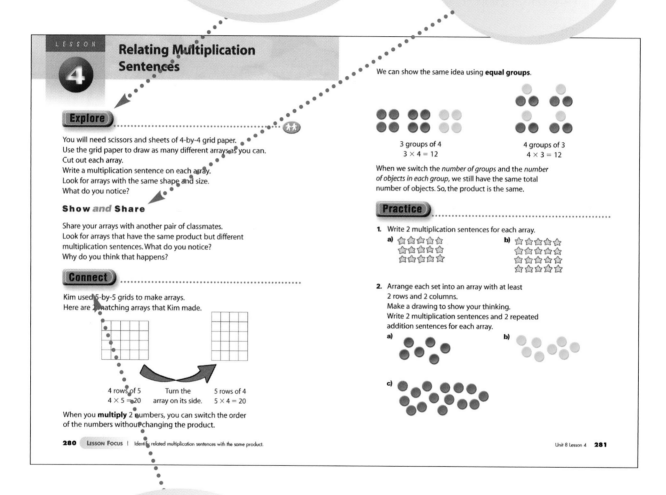

LESSON

4

Relating Multiplication Sentences

Explore

You will need scissors and sheets of 4-by-4 grid paper.
Use the grid paper to draw as many different arrays as you can.
Cut out each array.
Write a multiplication sentence on each array.
Look for arrays with the same shape and size.
What do you notice?

Show and Share

Share your arrays with another pair of classmates.
Look for arrays that have the same product but different
multiplication sentences. What do you notice?
Why do you think that happens?

Connect

Kim used 5-by-5 grids to make arrays.
Here are 2 matching arrays that Kim made.

4 rows of 5   Turn the   5 rows of 4
$4 \times 5 = 20$ array on its side. $5 \times 4 = 20$

When you **multiply** 2 numbers, you can switch the order
of the numbers without changing the product.

280 LESSON FOCUS | Identify related multiplication sentences with the same product.

We can show the same idea using **equal groups**.

3 groups of 4   4 groups of 3
$3 \times 4 = 12$ $4 \times 3 = 12$

When we switch the *number of groups* and the *number
of objects in each group*, we still have the same total
number of objects. So, the product is the same.

Practice

1. Write 2 multiplication sentences for each array.
   a)

   b)

2. Arrange each set into an array with at least
   2 rows and 2 columns.
   Make a drawing to show your thinking.
   Write 2 multiplication sentences and 2 repeated
   addition sentences for each array.
   a)

   b)

   c)

Unit 8 Lesson 4   **281**

Connect summarizes the math. It often shows a solution, or multiple solutions, to a question.

Practice questions help you to use and remember the math.

reminds you to use pictures, words, or numbers in your answers.

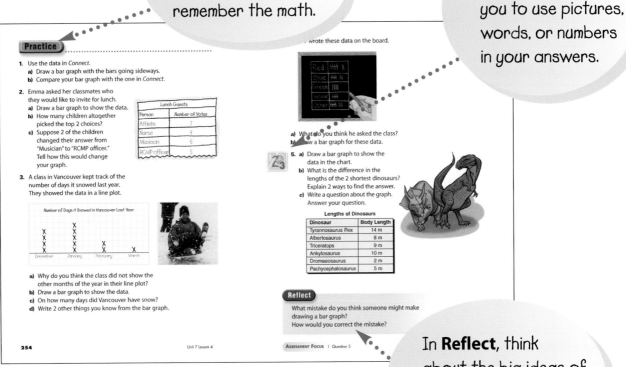

1. Use the data in *Connect*.
   a) Draw a bar graph with the bars going sideways.
   b) Compare your bar graph with the one in *Connect*.

2. Emma asked her classmates who they would like to invite for lunch.
   a) Draw a bar graph to show the data.
   b) How many children altogether picked the top 2 choices?
   c) Suppose 2 of the children changed their answer from "Musician" to "RCMP officer." Tell how this would change your graph.

Lunch Guests

Person	Number of Votes
Athlete	7
Nurse	4
Musician	6
RCMP officer	5

3. A class in Vancouver kept track of the number of days it snowed last year. They showed the data in a line plot.

Number of Days it Snowed in Vancouver Last Year

   a) Why do you think the class did not show the other months of the year in their line plot?
   b) Draw a bar graph to show the data.
   c) On how many days did Vancouver have snow?
   d) Write 2 other things you know from the bar graph.

...wrote these data on the board.

   a) What do you think he asked the class?
   b) Draw a bar graph for these data.

5. a) Draw a bar graph to show the data in the chart.
   b) What is the difference in the lengths of the 2 shortest dinosaurs? Explain 2 ways to find the answer.
   c) Write a question about the graph. Answer your question.

Lengths of Dinosaurs

Dinosaur	Body Length
Tyrannosaurus Rex	14 m
Albertosaurus	8 m
Triceratops	9 m
Ankylosaurus	10 m
Dromaeosaurus	2 m
Pachycephalosaurus	5 m

Reflect

What mistake do you think someone might make drawing a bar graph? How would you correct the mistake?

In **Reflect**, think about the big ideas of the lesson and about your learning style.

- Learn about strategies to help you solve problems in each **Strategies Toolkit** lesson.

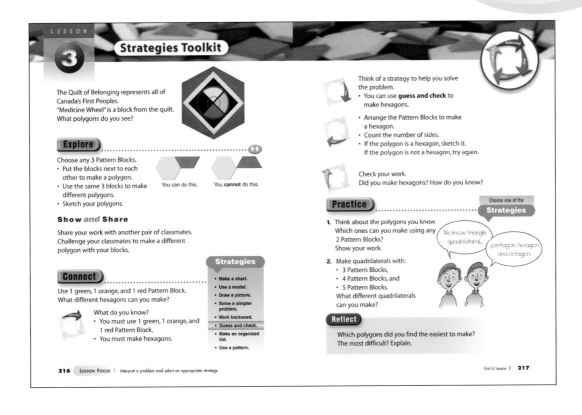

LESSON

3

Strategies Toolkit

The Quilt of Belonging represents all of Canada's First Peoples. "Medicine Wheel" is a block from the quilt. What polygons do you see?

Explore

Choose any 3 Pattern Blocks.
- Put the blocks next to each other to make a polygon.
- Use the same 3 blocks to make different polygons.
- Sketch your polygons.

You can do this.   You **cannot** do this.

Show and Share

Share your work with another pair of classmates. Challenge your classmates to make a different polygon with your blocks.

Connect

Use 1 green, 1 orange, and 1 red Pattern Block. What different hexagons can you make?

What do you know?
- You must use 1 green, 1 orange, and 1 red Pattern Block.
- You must make hexagons.

Strategies

- Make a chart.
- Use a model.
- Draw a picture.
- Solve a simpler problem.
- Work backward.
- Guess and check.
- Make an organized list.
- Use a pattern.

Think of a strategy to help you solve the problem.
- You can use **guess and check** to make hexagons.

- Arrange the Pattern Blocks to make a hexagon.
- Count the number of sides.
- If the polygon is a hexagon, sketch it. If the polygon is not a hexagon, try again.

Check your work. Did you make hexagons? How do you know?

Practice

Choose one of the **Strategies**

1. Think about the polygons you know. Which ones can you make using any 2 Pattern Blocks? Show your work.

   We know triangle, quadrilateral... ...pentagon, hexagon, and octagon.

2. Make quadrilaterals with:
   - 3 Pattern Blocks,
   - 4 Pattern Blocks, and
   - 5 Pattern Blocks.
   What different quadrilaterals can you make?

Reflect

Which polygons did you find the easiest to make? The most difficult? Explain.

- Check up on your learning in **Show What You Know** and **Cumulative Review**.

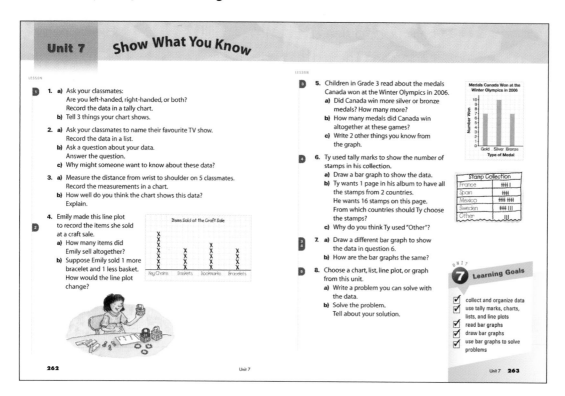

- The **Unit Problem** returns to the opening scene.

  It presents a problem to solve or a project to do using the math of the unit.

- Explore some interesting math when you do the **Investigations**.

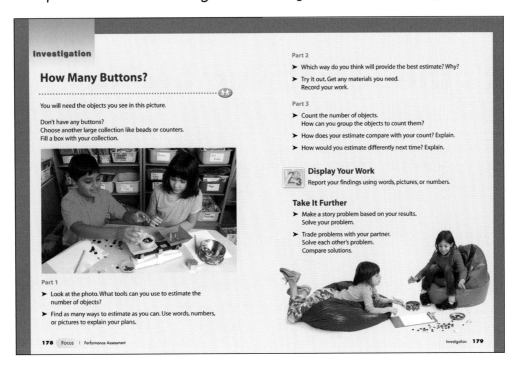

- You will see **Games** pages.

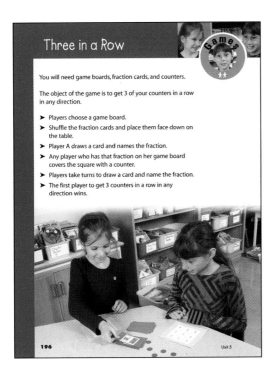

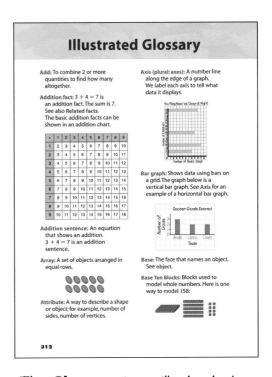

- The **Glossary** is an illustrated dictionary of important math words.

Investigation

What's the Secret Number?

Use materials such as counters or a hundred chart.

Part 1

Ed, Alecia, and Russell chose secret numbers.

My number is even. The tens digit is 1. The number of ones is greater than the sum of 2 and 4.

My number has 6 more tens than ones. The number of tens plus the number of ones is 12.

My number is between 26 and 54. You say my number when you count by 5s, but not when you count by 2s. My number does not have the same digits as 54.

➤ Find the secret numbers.

Part 2

Mia chose a secret number and gave these hints.

My secret number is an odd number. It is greater than 70.

➤ Did Mia give enough information? Explain.
➤ Mia's secret number is 87. What other hints could she give so a friend can find the secret number?
➤ Trade hints with another pair of classmates. Check each other's work.
➤ Talk about how different hints can describe the same number.

Part 3

➤ Choose a secret number less than 100.
➤ Write hints so someone could guess your number.
➤ Trade hints with another pair of classmates.
  Find their secret number.

Display Your Work

Make a poster for your secret number.
Put the hints on the front of the poster
and the number on the back.

Take It Further

Write a secret addition or subtraction sentence.
Make up hints about your sentence.
Read the hints to a classmate.
Have them guess your secret sentence.

Patterning

It's a Pattern Party!

Learning Goals

- identify, extend, create, and compare increasing patterns
- identify, extend, create, and compare decreasing patterns
- describe patterns and pattern rules
- use patterns to solve problems

growing patterns

increasing patterns

pattern rule

shrinking patterns

decreasing patterns

Children are wearing patterns, singing patterns, and dancing patterns. They are even clapping, tapping, and snapping patterns.

- What patterns do you see in the picture?
- Think about making a dancing pattern. What might it be?
- Think about making a sound pattern. How would it sound?

Exploring Increasing Patterns

Here is a **growing pattern**.

Figure 1

Figure 2

Figure 3

Figure 4

What stays the same and what changes in each figure?
What will Figure 5 look like?

You will need Pattern Blocks.

➤ Show what Figure 4 looks like.

➤ Now make Figure 5 and Figure 6.

Figure 1

Show **and** Share

Show your patterns to another pair of classmates. Take turns describing the patterns.

Figure 2

Figure 3

LESSON FOCUS | Identify, describe, and extend increasing patterns.

Growing patterns are **increasing patterns**.

➤ This pattern grows by the same number of blocks each time.

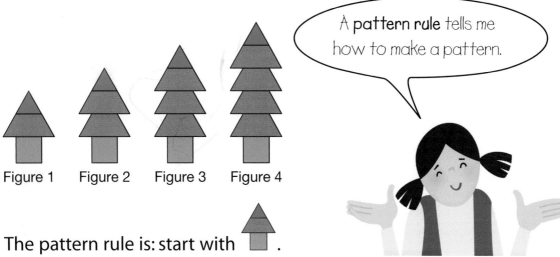

A pattern rule tells me how to make a pattern.

Figure 1   Figure 2   Figure 3   Figure 4

The pattern rule is: start with ▲.

Put in 1 more ◸ each time.

➤ This pattern grows by a different number of blocks each time.

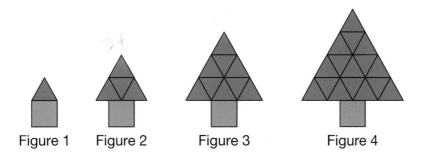

Figure 1   Figure 2   Figure 3   Figure 4

The pattern rule is:

• Start with ▲.
• Add 3 ▲s to make a larger triangle.
• Then, add 2 more ▲s than the time before. Keep the triangular tree shape each time.

What will Figure 5 look like?
Add ▲ blocks to make the tree larger.

1. Use Pattern Blocks.
   Make the next 3 figures in each increasing pattern.

   a)

   Figure 1   Figure 2   Figure 3

   b)

   Figure 1   Figure 2   Figure 3

   c)

   Figure 1   Figure 2   Figure 3

2. Write the pattern rule for each pattern in question 1.

 3. Use Pattern Blocks.
   Copy the pattern.
   Make the next 3 figures.
   Draw the pattern on grid paper.
   Write the pattern rule.

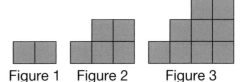

Figure 1   Figure 2   Figure 3

4. Sammi drew this increasing pattern.
   His pattern grows by the same number each time.

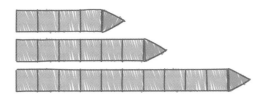

   Is a figure missing? If so, draw it.

Reflect

Choose an increasing pattern from this lesson.
Tell how it grows.

Creating Increasing Patterns

A sign store makes letters that come in different sizes.
Here are the first 3 sizes of the letter U.

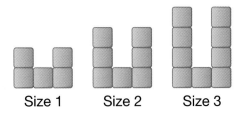

Size 1   Size 2   Size 3

What does the next letter in the pattern look like?
What is the pattern rule?

Explore

You will need square tiles and grid paper.

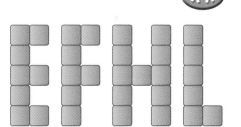

➤ Choose 1 of these letters.

➤ Use square tiles to make the letter.

➤ Create an increasing pattern to show the letter in 3 more sizes.

➤ Draw the pattern on grid paper.

➤ Repeat this activity with a different letter.

Show and Share

Share the letters you made with another pair of classmates.
Take turns describing each other's pattern rule.

To make an increasing pattern you:
• create a starting point
• decide what to change each time

Liam and Maya are making the letter T for the sign store.

➤ Liam chose this pattern rule:
  • Start with ⊤. Add 1 ▢ each time.
  His pattern grows in 1 direction.

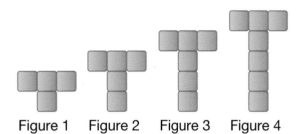

Figure 1   Figure 2   Figure 3   Figure 4

An increasing pattern can grow in different ways.

➤ Maya chose this pattern rule:
  • Start with ⊤. Add 3 ▢s each time, one at each end of the T-shape.
  Her pattern grows in more than 1 direction.

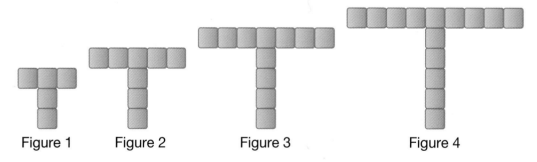

Figure 1   Figure 2   Figure 3   Figure 4

Math Link

Social Studies

Inuit use patterns on kamiks (boots) to show gender. Females' kamiks have horizontal bands. Males' kamiks have vertical bands.

1. Use square tiles.
   Make a pattern that uses this rule:
   Start with 4 squares. Add 2 squares each time.
   Draw the pattern on grid paper.
   Describe your pattern using numbers and words.

2. Write an increasing pattern rule.
   Trade pattern rules with a classmate.
   Make your classmate's pattern.
   Check each other's work.

3. Draw the first 4 figures of an increasing pattern.
   Write about your pattern.

4. Figure 3 is missing.
   Sketch what it should be.
   Explain how you know.

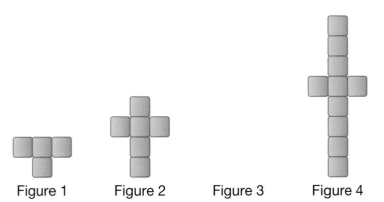

| Figure 1 | Figure 2 | Figure 3 | Figure 4 |

5. a) Use 2 or more actions to make an increasing pattern.
   b) Record the pattern rule.
   c) Clap, snap, or stomp the pattern.

Reflect

Explain the steps you take to make an increasing pattern.

Comparing Increasing Patterns

 **Explore** ●●●●●●●●●●●●●●●●●●●●●●●●●●●●●●●●●●●●

You will need square tiles and grid paper.

➤ Use the starting point shown here.

➤ Make an increasing pattern that grows by 1 ■ each time.

➤ Make an increasing pattern that grows by 2 ■s each time.

➤ Draw your patterns on grid paper.

Show *and* Share

Share your patterns with another pair of classmates.
How are the patterns the same? How are they different?

Connect ●●●●●●●●●●●●●●●●●●●●●●●●●●●●●●●●●●●●●●●

➤ Carly made this pattern.

Figure 1   Figure 2   Figure 3   Figure 4   Figure 5

Sam made this pattern.

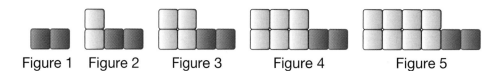

Figure 1   Figure 2   Figure 3   Figure 4   Figure 5

The patterns use the same starting point but they increase
in different ways.

Carly's pattern rule is:

• Start with ■■■. Add 1 □ at the end each time.

Sam's pattern rule is:

• Start with ■■■. Add □ at the front each time.

➤ Eli made this pattern.

Figure 1   Figure 2   Figure 3   Figure 4

Pona made this pattern.

Figure 1   Figure 2   Figure 3   Figure 4

Their patterns use different starting points but they increase the same way.

Eli's pattern rule is:

• Start with ▦. Add a ☐ at each end each time.

Pona's pattern rule is:

• Start with ▦. Add a ☐ at each end each time.

1. **a)** Write the pattern rule.

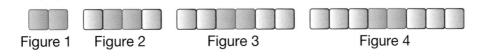

Figure 1   Figure 2   Figure 3   Figure 4

b) Draw a pattern that has the same starting point but increases a different way.

2. Which 2 patterns have different starting points but increase the same way? Write the pattern rule for each.

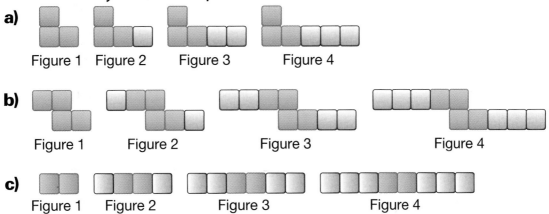

a)

Figure 1   Figure 2   Figure 3   Figure 4

b)

Figure 1   Figure 2   Figure 3   Figure 4

c)

Figure 1   Figure 2   Figure 3   Figure 4

3. Make an increasing pattern. Show the first 4 figures.
Compare your pattern with that of a classmate.
Write about the patterns using numbers and words.
How are the patterns the same? How are they different?

4. Jess made this pattern.

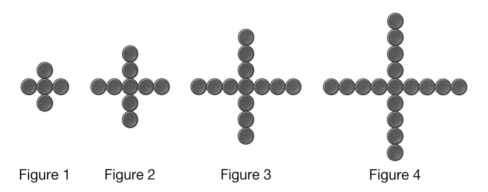

Figure 1   Figure 2   Figure 3   Figure 4

Molly made this pattern.

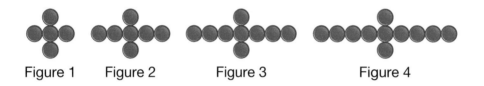

Figure 1   Figure 2   Figure 3   Figure 4

How are the patterns the same? How are they different?
Write the pattern rule for each pattern.

5. Use square tiles.
   a) Start with 3 ⬜s. Add 1 ⬜ each
   time to make a pattern.
   b) Repeat part a, but make a
   different pattern.
   c) Compare your patterns with
   those of a classmate.
   How are they the same?
   How are they different?

Reflect

How can you compare increasing patterns?

Increasing Number Patterns

How would you count the eyes in this group of children? How would you count the number of fingers on the raised hands?

Explore

You will need a hundred chart from 1 to 100 and 2 colours of markers or crayons.

➤ How can you use the hundred chart to count by 2s? By 5s?

➤ Colour to record your work. What patterns do you see?

1	2	3	4	5	6	7	8	9	10
11	12	13	14	15	16	17	18	19	20
21	22	23	24	25	26	27	28	29	30
31	32	33	34	35	36	37	38	39	40
41	42	43	44	45	46	47	48	49	50
51	52	53	54	55	56	57	58	59	60
61	62	63	64	65	66	67	68	69	70
71	72	73	74	75	76	77	78	79	80
81	82	83	84	85	86	87	88	89	90
91	92	93	94	95	96	97	98	99	100

Show *and* Share

Compare your patterns with those of another pair of classmates.
Which numbers are shaded twice? Why do you think that happens?

Connect

The numbers in the coloured squares form an increasing pattern.

1	2	3	4	5	6	7	8	9	10
11	12	13	14	15	16	17	18	19	20
21	22	23	24	25	26	27	28	29	30
31	32	33	34	35	36	37	38	39	40
41	42	43	44	45	46	47	48	49	50
51	52	53	54	55	56	57	58	59	60
61	62	63	64	65	66	67	68	69	70
71	72	73	74	75	76	77	78	79	80
81	82	83	84	85	86	87	88	89	90
91	92	93	94	95	96	97	98	99	100

The numbers in the yellow squares end in 0. The numbers in the blue squares end in 5.

➤ The pattern rule for the yellow squares is:
- Start at 10. Add 10 each time.

The pattern makes 1 vertical line.
The tens digit increases by 1. The ones digit is always 0.

➤ The pattern rule for the blue squares is:
- Start at 5. Add 10 each time.

The pattern makes 1 vertical line.
The tens digit increases by 1. The ones digit is always 5.

1. Describe this pattern using numbers and words.

1	2	3	4	5	6	7	8	9	10
11	12	13	14	15	16	17	18	19	20

2. Réjean started a number pattern.
   Which numbers would you shade to
   extend the pattern?
   What is the pattern rule?

1	2	3	4	5	6	7	8	9	10
11	12	13	14	15	16	17	18	19	20
21	22	23	24	25	26	27	28	29	30
31	32	33	34	35	36	37	38	39	40
41	42	43	44	45	46	47	48	49	50
51	52	53	54	55	56	57	58	59	60
61	62	63	64	65	66	67	68	69	70
71	72	73	74	75	76	77	78	79	80
81	82	83	84	85	86	87	88	89	90
91	92	93	94	95	96	97	98	99	100

3. Use a hundred chart from 1 to 100.
   a) Start at 30. Add 10 each time.
      Shade the numbers in this
      pattern blue.
   b) Find a different number pattern
      on the same hundred chart.
      Shade the numbers in this pattern red.
   c) Compare the patterns.

4. Copy each pattern. Write the pattern rule.
   Fill in the missing numbers.
   a) 15, 20, 25, ____, ____, ____
   b) 40, 50, 60, ____, ____, ____

5. Jess is counting her coins.
   She says, "25, 30, 35, 40, 45, 50. I have 50 cents!"
   Describe the pattern using numbers.
   What coins do you think she has? Explain.

Reflect

Choose a number pattern from this lesson.
Describe the strategy you use to find the pattern rule.
Use words and numbers to explain.

Strategies Toolkit

Explore

Joe is building this tower using Pattern Blocks.
Each level has 1 red block and 2 orange blocks.
He has lots of red blocks, but only 10 orange blocks.
How many levels of the tower can he build?

Work together to solve this problem.
Use any materials you think will help.

Show *and* Share

Tell about the strategy you used to solve this problem.

Connect

Jaleel is stacking Pattern Blocks.
Each level has these blocks.
She has 23 green blocks and 15 red blocks.
How many levels can she make?
Will she have any blocks left over?

Strategies

- **Make a chart.**
- **Use a model.**
- **Draw a picture.**
- **Solve a simpler problem.**
- **Work backward.**
- **Guess and test.**
- **Make an organized list.**
- **Use a pattern.**

Understand

What do you know?
- There are 23 green blocks and 15 red blocks.
- There are 3 green blocks and 1 red block in each level.

Plan

Think of a strategy to help you solve the problem.
- You can **use a pattern**.

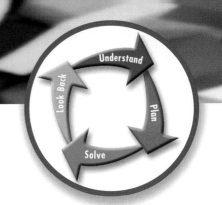

Use a hundred chart from 1 to 100
to record the pattern.
Shade the numbers of green blocks
used at each level.
How many levels can you build before
you run out of green blocks?
Are there enough red blocks to build that many levels?

Check your work.
How could you solve this problem another way?

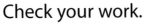

Practice

Choose one of the
Strategies

1. Hakim builds a tower with yellow blocks and
   orange blocks. There are 5 levels in the tower.
   Each level has 2 yellow blocks and 3 orange blocks.
   How many orange blocks and yellow blocks
   are in his tower?

2. Sari made a chart that shows the total number
   of blocks in each level of her tower.
   What is the total number of blocks in Level 6?
   How do you know?

Level	Total Number of Blocks
1	18
2	22
3	26

Reflect

How can you use a pattern to help you solve a problem?
Use words, numbers, or pictures to explain.

What's the Pattern Rule?

You will need square tiles, Build Pattern cards, and Starting Point cards.

The object of the game is to guess your partner's pattern rule.

- Shuffle both sets of cards and place them face down.

- Select a Starting Point card. Place it face up in front of you.

- Select a Build Pattern card. Keep it a secret.

- Use the starting point and the build pattern rule.
  Make the first 5 figures of an increasing pattern.

- Take turns describing each other's pattern rules.
  If you describe your partner's pattern rule correctly,
  you score 1 point. If not, your partner scores a point.

- Draw new cards and play again.

- The player with the higher score after 3 rounds wins.

Exploring Decreasing Patterns

Jay has eggs for breakfast every day.

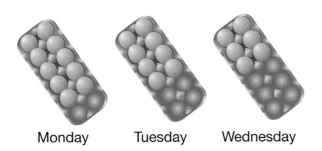

Monday   Tuesday   Wednesday

How many eggs will there be after breakfast on Thursday?
How do you know?

Explore

You will need Snap Cubes.

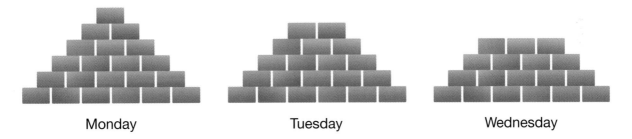

Monday   Tuesday   Wednesday

Workers take bricks from the pile every day.

➤ Show what the pile of bricks will look like on Thursday.

➤ Show what they will look like on Friday and Saturday.

Show *and* Share

Show your piles of Snap Cubes to another pair of classmates.
Take turns describing the pattern rule.

Connect

Shrinking patterns are **decreasing patterns**.

➤ Maxwell's tennis class starts with 15 balls.
They lose the same number of balls each class.

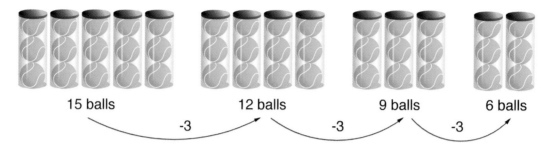

15 balls   12 balls   9 balls   6 balls
        -3   -3   -3

The numbers of balls are 15, 12, 9, 6, …
The pattern rule is:

• Start with 15 balls. Remove 3 balls each time.

Increasing patterns grow.
Decreasing patterns shrink.

➤ Chloe's tennis class starts with 15 balls. They lose
a different number of balls each class.

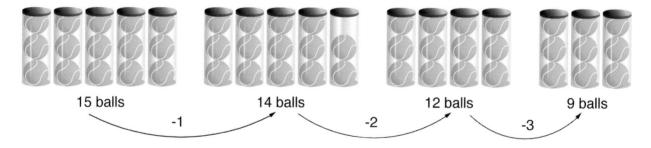

15 balls   14 balls   12 balls   9 balls
        -1   -2   -3

The numbers of balls are 15, 14, 12, 9, …
The pattern rule is:

• Start with 15 balls. Remove 1 ball.

• Then, remove 1 more ball than the time before.

1. Use Snap Cubes.
   Make the next 3 figures in each decreasing pattern.

   a)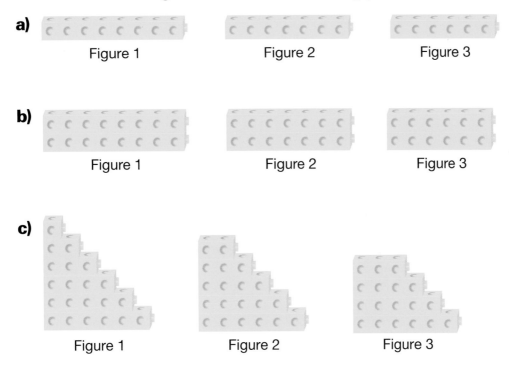

   b)

   c)

2. Look at the patterns in question 1.
   Write the pattern rule for each.

3. Janie made a decreasing pattern out of beads.
   She continues the pattern.
   How many more figures can she make?
   Explain how you know.

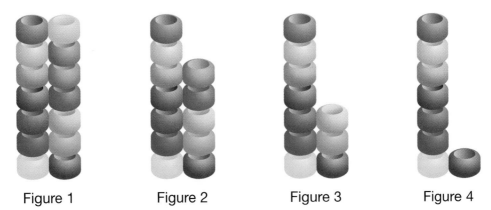

4. Zin photographed birds while he was camping.
He arranged the photographs to make a decreasing pattern.

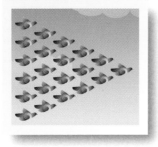
Figure 1

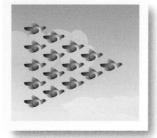
Figure 2

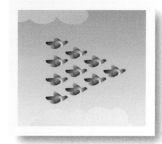
Figure 3

Which picture below extends the pattern?
Tell how you know.

a)

b)

5. A grocery clerk has 28 cereal boxes.
She continues this pattern.

The clerk uses all the boxes.
How many boxes will be in the top row?
How do you know? Sketch the display.

At Home

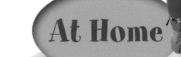

Reflect

Choose a decreasing pattern
from this lesson.
Tell how it shrinks.

Be a pattern detective!
Look for patterns on clothing,
buildings, furniture, or wallpaper.
What patterns can you find?

Creating and Comparing Decreasing Patterns

Professor Shrinker built a shrinking machine.
She put a necklace through the machine 3 times.

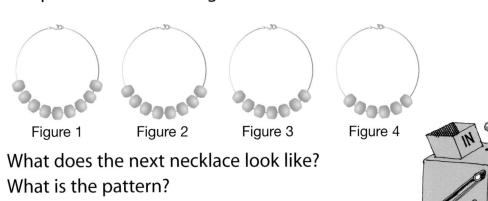

| Figure 1 | Figure 2 | Figure 3 | Figure 4 |

What does the next necklace look like?
What is the pattern?

 **Explore**

You will need counters.

➤ Make a caterpillar with 10 to 15 counters.

➤ Create a decreasing pattern to show the caterpillar in 4 different sizes.

➤ Draw the pattern.
Record the pattern rule.

➤ Repeat the activity with a different pattern rule.

Show *and* Share

Compare your caterpillar with that of another pair of classmates.
Take turns describing each other's pattern rule.

 **LESSON FOCUS** | Create, describe, and compare decreasing patterns. **25**

To make a decreasing pattern you:
* create a starting point
* decide what to remove each time

➤ Ellis chose this pattern rule:
  * Start with 11 ▲s in a line. Remove 2 ▲s each time.

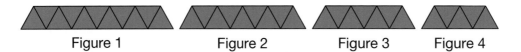

Figure 1   Figure 2   Figure 3   Figure 4

➤ Julie chose this pattern rule:
  * Start with 11 ▲s in a line. Remove 1 ▲.
  * Then, remove 1 more ▲ than the time before.

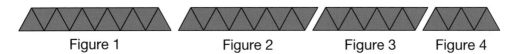

Figure 1   Figure 2   Figure 3   Figure 4

Their patterns have the same starting point but they decrease in different ways.

Practice

1. Stewie's pattern train started with 20 blocks. He removed 2 blocks at each step of his pattern. Make a pattern that follows the same pattern rule. Describe your pattern using numbers and words.

2. How are these patterns the same? How are they different?
   Tell the pattern rule for each.

a)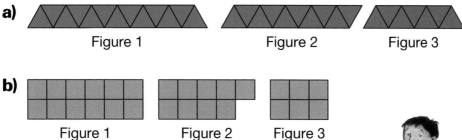

Figure 1   Figure 2   Figure 3

b)

Figure 1   Figure 2   Figure 3

3. Use 2 or more actions to
   make a decreasing pattern.
   Describe the pattern rule.
   Clap, snap, or stomp your pattern.

4. Professor Shrinker put a creature in her shrinking machine.
   Draw or make the missing creature.
   Tell the pattern rule.

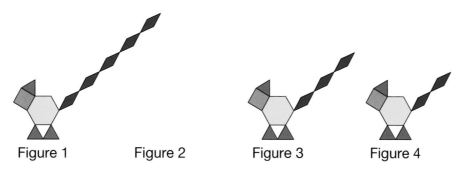

Figure 1   Figure 2   Figure 3   Figure 4

5. Make a decreasing pattern. Show the first 4 figures.
   Compare your pattern with that of a classmate.
   Record how the patterns are the same and
   how they are different.

Reflect

Explain the steps you take to make
a decreasing pattern.

Decreasing Number Patterns

Carly has 20¢. Each day she buys a sticker for 2¢.

Will she ever have 9¢? How do you know?

Explore

You will need a hundred chart from 100 to 1 and markers or crayons.

Suppose you have 95¢.
Prizes cost 5¢ each.
How many prizes can you buy?

➤ Record your work on the hundred chart.

➤ What pattern do you see?

Show *and* Share

Compare your number pattern with that of another pair of classmates.
Decide on the pattern rule.

100	99	98	97	96	95	94	93	92	91
90	89	88	87	86	85	84	83	82	81
80	79	78	77	76	75	74	73	72	71
70	69	68	67	66	65	64	63	62	61
60	59	58	57	56	55	54	53	52	51
50	49	48	47	46	45	44	43	42	41
40	39	38	37	36	35	34	33	32	31
30	29	28	27	26	25	24	23	22	21
20	19	18	17	16	15	14	13	12	11
10	9	8	7	6	5	4	3	2	1

The numbers in the coloured squares form patterns.

The pattern rule for the orange squares is:
• Start at 100. Count back by 5s each time.

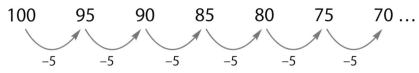

100   95   90   85   80   75   70 …
   −5   −5   −5   −5   −5   −5

The ones digit follows this pattern: 0, 5, 0, 5, 0, 5, …
The tens digit follows this pattern: 9, 9, 8, 8, 7, 7, …

The pattern rule for the green squares is:
• Start at 100. Count back by 2s each time.

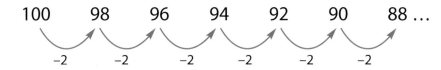

100   98   96   94   92   90   88 …
   −2   −2   −2   −2   −2   −2

The ones digit follows this pattern: 8, 6, 4, 2, 0, 8, 6, 4, 2, 0, …
The tens digit follows this pattern: 9, 9, 9, 9, 9, 8, 8, 8, 8, 8, 7, 7, 7, 7, 7, …

Both patterns form vertical lines.
Some numbers appear in both patterns.

1. Write the first 4 numbers in each pattern.
   a) Start at 75. Count back 5 each time.
   b) Start at 100. Count back 3 each time.
   c) Start at 65. Count back 10 each time.
   d) Start at 50. Count back 2 each time.

2. May-Lin coloured these patterns on a
   hundred chart from 100 to 1.

100	99	98	97	96	95	94	93	92	91
90	89	88	87	86	85	84	83	82	81
80	79	78	77	76	75	74	73	72	71
70	69	68	67	66	65	64	63	62	61
60	59	58	57	56	55	54	53	52	51
50	49	48	47	46	45	44	43	42	41
40	39	38	37	36	35	34	33	32	31
30	29	28	27	26	25	24	23	22	21
20	19	18	17	16	15	14	13	12	11
10	9	8	7	6	5	4	3	2	1

Describe the patterns.
How are they the same? How are they different?

3. Copy each pattern.
   Write the pattern rule.
   Fill in the missing numbers.
   a) 78, 76, 74, 72, ___, ___, ___
   b) 35, 30, 25, 20, ___, ___, ___
   c) 100, 90, 80, ___, ___, ___, ___
   d) 83, 80, 77, ___, ___, ___, ___

4. Elise wrote this number pattern: 98, 96, 94, 92, 88, 86
   Is she missing any numbers?
   How do you know?

5. Suppose you write this pattern: 74, 72, 70, 68, …
   Will you write 47?
   How do you know?

6. Use this hundred chart.

100	99	98	97	96	95	94	93	92	91
90	89	88	87	86	85	84	83	82	81
80	79	78	77	76	75	74	73	72	71
70	69	68	67	66	65	64	63	62	61
60	59	58	57	56	55	54	53	52	51
50	49	48	47	46	45	44	43	42	41
40	39	38	37	36	35	34	33	32	31
30	29	28	27	26	25	24	23	22	21
20	19	18	17	16	15	14	13	12	11
10	9	8	7	6	5	4	3	2	1

a) The coloured squares form a decreasing pattern.
Tell the pattern rule.

b) Will the number 18 be in this pattern?
How do you know?

c) Extend the pattern to find out.

7. Shade a decreasing number pattern on a hundred chart
from 100 to 1.
Tell the pattern rule.
Compare your pattern with that of a classmate.
How are the patterns the same?
How are they different?

8. Salvio had 18 apples.
Each day he ate 2 apples.
How many apples did Salvio have after
5 days?

Reflect

How is a decreasing pattern the same as an
increasing pattern?
How is it different?
Give examples to explain your thinking.

LESSON

1

1. Draw the next 3 figures in each increasing pattern.

a)   **b)**

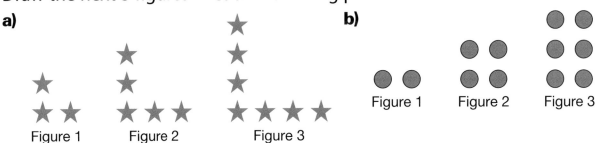

2. Write the pattern rule for each pattern in question 1.

2

3. Use this picture as the starting point.
Write a pattern rule.
Draw the next 4 figures
in the pattern.

3

4. Write the pattern rule for each pattern.
How are the patterns the same? How are they different?

a)

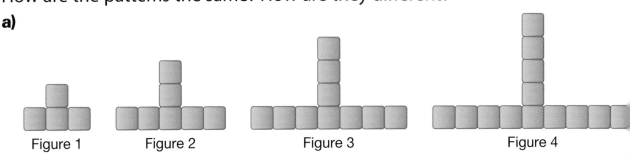

b)

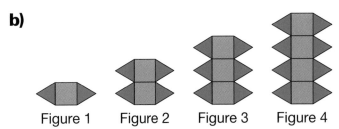

5. Jez wrote this pattern: 15, 20, 25, 30, 35
   a) Write the pattern rule.
   b) Write the next 3 numbers in the pattern.
   c) Choose a different start number.
      Write a different pattern that grows the same way.

6. Use grid paper.
   Draw the next 3 figures in this pattern.
   Write the pattern rule.

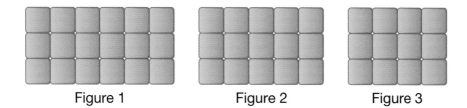

Figure 1   Figure 2   Figure 3

7. Choose a starting point. Make a decreasing pattern.
   Draw 4 figures of your pattern.
   Compare your pattern with that of a classmate.
   How are the patterns the same?
   How are they different?

8. Look at these number patterns.
   i) 22, 20, 18, 16, 14   **ii)** 60, 55, 50, 45
      a) Write the pattern rule for each
         number pattern.
      b) How are the patterns the same?
         How are they different?
      c) Write the next 3 numbers
         in each pattern.
      d) Write a number pattern that
         decreases in a different way.

UNIT

1 **Learning Goals**

✓ identify, extend, create, and compare increasing patterns

✓ identify, extend, create, and compare decreasing patterns

✓ describe patterns and pattern rules

✓ use patterns to solve problems

It's a Pattern Party!

The class is making patterns for the pattern party.
They are making increasing and decreasing patterns.

Part 1

●●○   ●●○○   ●●○○○   ●●○○○○

Figure 1   Figure 2   Figure 3   Figure 4

Each ● means clap your hands.
Each ○ means stamp your feet.
➤ Write the pattern rule.
➤ Draw the next 3 figures.
➤ Clap and stamp the pattern.

Part 2

➤ Make a sound or action pattern for the party.
   It can be an increasing or a decreasing pattern.
➤ Draw your pattern.
➤ Write about your pattern.
➤ Try your pattern.

Part 3

The pattern party needs decorations!

➤ Draw an increasing or decreasing pattern.
➤ Write about your pattern.
➤ Tell how to extend your pattern.
➤ Display your pattern in the classroom.

Reflect on Your Learning

Think about the different increasing and decreasing patterns you made in this unit.
Write 2 things you learned about these kinds of patterns.

UNIT 2

Numbers to

The Market

Learning Goals

- model, compare, and order numbers to 1000
- explore the meaning of place value for numbers to 1000
- skip count by 3s, 4s, 5s, 10s, 25s, and 100s
- estimate a quantity using a referent

1000

Key Words

standard form

digit

place value

compare

order

number line

estimate

referent

thousand

Saturday morning at the market you will find vegetables and fruits fresh from the fields, bread and bannock to sample, and lots of fun things to make and do!

Hayride tickets

$3 - children
$5 - adults

Rides Today

364

Look at the picture.

• How are numbers used at the market?

• What is the greatest number you can find in the picture?

• What story can you tell about this number?

Counting Large Collections

Counting beyond 100 uses the same patterns as counting to 100.

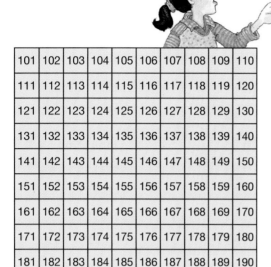

101	102	103	104	105	106	107	108	109	110
111	112	113	114	115	116	117	118	119	120
121	122	123	124	125	126	127	128	129	130
131	132	133	134	135	136	137	138	139	140
141	142	143	144	145	146	147	148	149	150
151	152	153	154	155	156	157	158	159	160
161	162	163	164	165	166	167	168	169	170
171	172	173	174	175	176	177	178	179	180
181	182	183	184	185	186	187	188	189	190
191	192	193	194	195	196	197	198	199	200

Starting at one hundred eight,
108, 109, 110, 111, 112, 113, 114, …

Starting at one hundred forty-six,
146, 147, 148, 149, 150, 151, 152, …

What numbers come after 199?
After 209?

Explore

Choose a collection of objects.

Group the objects, then count them.
Find a different way to group the objects. Count again.
Record your work.

Show *and* Share

Show your collection to another group.
Explain how grouping helped you count the objects.
Discuss other ways you could group the objects.

One way to count a large collection is
to make groups of tens and hundreds.

➤ Count the straws.
There is one group of 100,
one group of 10, and three 1s.

First count the hundreds, then
count on the tens and the ones.

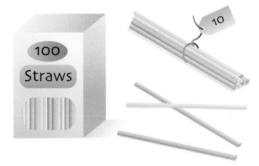

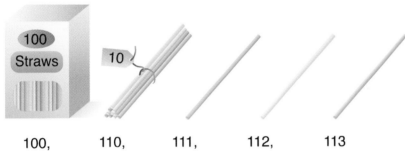

100,   110,   111,   112,   113

There are one hundred thirteen straws.

➤ Count the buttons.
There are 2 bags of 100 buttons, 3 cups of 10 buttons,
and 4 single buttons.

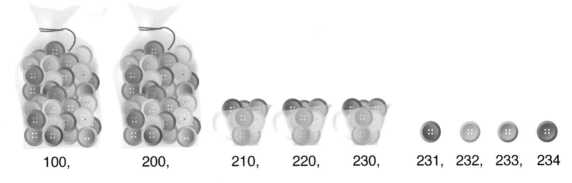

100,   200,   210,   220,   230,   231, 232, 233, 234

There are two hundred thirty-four buttons.

➤ Draw a collection of 317 buttons.

 Think: I need to draw 3 bags of 100 buttons, 1 cup of 10 buttons, and 7 single buttons.

Count to check: 100, 200, 300, 310, 311, 312, 313, 314, 315, 316, 317

1. How many? Record your count.

a)

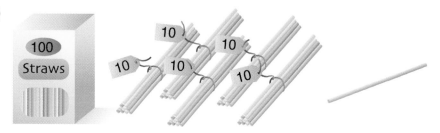

b)

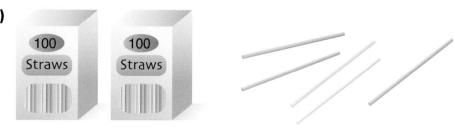

2. Draw pictures to represent each number.
Tell the number of hundreds, tens, and ones.

a) 139   **b)** 224   **c)** 120   **d)** 73

3. Why do we use groups of tens and hundreds to help count large collections?

4. Draw a collection of 333 objects.
Use your drawing to explain the meaning of each digit in the number 333.

5. Céline counted the pennies in her bank but she knows she isn't right.
Find her mistake and correct the count.

217, 218, 219,
300, 301, 302

6. Copy the rows of this hundred chart.
Fill in the missing numbers.

101	102	103	104	105				109	
	112	113			116	117	118		
		123	124	125	126	127	128		

7. Michael filled in this row of a hundred chart.
Find the mistakes he made.
What numbers belong in those spaces?

| 251 | 252 | 253 | 254 | 255 | 265 | 257 | 258 | 259 | 270 |

Reflect

Explain one way to make counting large collections easier.

At Home

Find a large collection. Count how many objects are in the collection.

Modelling 3-Digit Numbers

A farmer harvests 128 ears of corn.

You can use pictures to show this number.

You can use Base Ten Blocks to model this number.

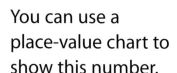

You can use a place-value chart to show this number.

Hundreds	Tens	Ones
1	2	8

Explore

You will need Base Ten Blocks and a place-value chart.

➤ Choose a secret number between 100 and 1000. Model it with Base Ten Blocks.

➤ Have your partner tell what the number is, and write it in a place-value chart.

➤ Switch roles. Repeat this activity 5 times.

Show and Share

Tell your partner how you knew what to write in the place-value chart.

Our number system is based on groups of 10.

 100 one hundred 1 hundred = 10 tens	10 ten 1 ten = 10 ones	1 one

Here is one way to model 432.

4 hundreds   3 tens   2 ones

Hundreds	Tens	Ones
4	3	2

The value of this digit is 4 hundreds, or 400.

The value of this digit is 3 tens, or 30.

The value of this digit is 2 ones, or 2.

We can think of 432 as 400 + 30 + 2.
The base-ten name is 4 hundreds 3 tens 2 ones.
In words: four hundred thirty-two

Here is a way to show 205.

The 0 in 205 tells we can model the number using no tens.

Hundreds	Tens	Ones
2	0	5

The base-ten name is 2 hundreds 5 ones.
In words: two hundred five

· ·

1. Use a place-value chart to show each number. Write the number.

   a)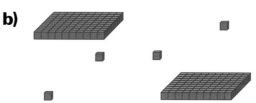

   b)

2. Draw a picture to show each number.
   a) 417 b) 540 c) 966 d) 795 e) 128 f) 702

3. Write the base-ten name for each number.
   a) 582 b) 414 c) 690 d) 308 e) 500 f) 987

4. Write the number for each base-ten name.
   a) 9 hundreds 6 tens 2 ones   b) 7 hundreds 8 tens
   c) 5 hundreds 7 ones   d) 8 hundreds 8 tens 8 ones

5. Give the value of each underlined digit.
   a) 8<u>5</u>4   b) <u>7</u>15   c) 10<u>9</u>   d) <u>5</u>26
   e) 7<u>0</u>8   f) 33<u>9</u>   g) 35<u>0</u>   h) 6<u>8</u>8

6. a) How many ones make 1 ten?
   b) How many tens make 1 hundred?
   c) How many hundreds make 1 thousand?
   d) What pattern do you see?
   e) How many thousands make 10 000? Explain.

7. Draw Base Ten Blocks to show each answer.
   a) Which number is 10 more than 167?
   b) Which number is 3 less than 348?
   c) Which number is 200 more than 203?

Reflect

How does the value of each digit in 747
depend on its place in the number?
Use words, pictures, or numbers to explain.

Showing Numbers in Many Ways

Sam and Jamie use Base Ten Blocks
to model the number 34.

Sam: 3 tens 4 ones   Jamie: 2 tens 14 ones

What other ways can you model 34 with Base Ten Blocks?

Explore

You will need Base Ten Blocks, a pencil, and paper.

➤ Show 236 in 3 different ways with Base Ten Blocks.
   Record each way.
   Use pictures, words, and numbers.

Show and Share

Talk about the different ways you modelled the number.

Connect

Here are different ways to show 208.
When you use digits, the number is written in **standard form:** 208

Picture: ⬜ ⬜ • • • • • • •

Base-ten name: 2 hundreds 8 ones

Place-value chart:

Hundreds	Tens	Ones
2	0	8

Base Ten Blocks:

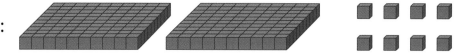

You can also show 208 as

   or as

1 hundred 10 tens 8 ones   1 hundred 9 tens 18 ones

Practice

Use Base Ten Blocks when they help.

1. Write the base-ten name for each number.

a)

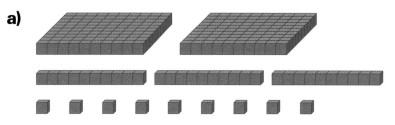

b) 862   **c)** 501   **d)** twenty-seven

2. Write each number in standard form.

a)

b)
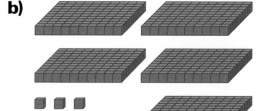

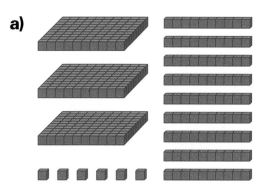

c) sixty-seven   **d)** 6 hundreds 8 tens
e) ninety-four   **f)** 3 hundreds 4 tens 5 ones

3. Draw Base Ten Blocks to show each number using the fewest blocks. Write each number in standard form.

a)

b)

4. Show each number in 3 different ways.
   a) 286   **b)** 309   **c)** 529

   Compare your ways with those of your classmates.
   What do you notice?

5. Draw Base Ten Blocks to show each number in 3 different ways.
   a) 61   **b)** 315   **c)** 406

6. What does the zero in 308 mean?

7. Draw Base Ten Blocks.
   Show 267 using exactly 24 blocks.
   Explain how you did it.

8. Ellen says that there are 53 tens in 536.
   Do you agree? Explain your thinking.

Reflect

How do you know that both pictures show 241? Use words, numbers, or pictures to explain.

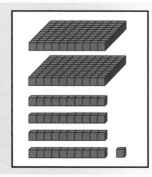
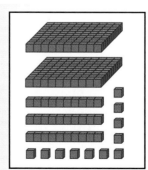

Strategies Toolkit

Explore

How many 3-digit numbers can you build using any 4 of these blocks for each number?

Show your work.

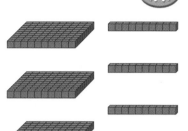

Show *and* Share

Show your classmates how you made the numbers.

Connect

How many 3-digit numbers can you build using any 3 of these blocks for each number?

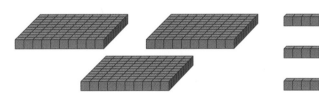

Strategies

- Make a table.
- Use a model.
- Draw a picture.
- Solve a simpler problem.
- Work backward.
- Guess and test.
- **Make an organized list.**
- Use a pattern.

What do you know?
- You have to build as many 3-digit numbers as you can.
- You may use only 3 blocks to build each number.

Think of a strategy to help you solve the problem.
- You can **make an organized list**.
- List all the numbers with 3 hundreds, then 2 hundreds, then 1 hundred.

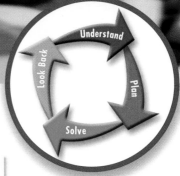

Make a chart to record your list.

Hundreds	Tens	Ones	Number

- Start with 3 hundreds.
  How many numbers can you build?
  Record this in the chart.
- Repeat with 2 hundreds, then 1 hundred.

How do you know you have found all the numbers?
What other way could you solve the problem?

Practice

Choose one of the Strategies

1. Use any number of these blocks to make as many numbers as you can.

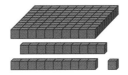

2. Roll a number cube 3 times.
   Use the numbers rolled to make as many 3-digit numbers as you can.

3. Balloons come in packages of 10, 25, and 50.
   You need 150 balloons.
   Find 5 ways you could buy the balloons.

Reflect

Choose a *Practice* question.
How did you make an organized list to solve the problem?
Use words, pictures, or numbers to explain.

LESSON 5

Comparing and Ordering Numbers

Who Has the Greatest Number?

You will need a game board for each player and 4 sets of cards numbered 0 to 9. Shuffle the cards and place them face down.

➤ Each player makes a 3-digit number. Follow these steps.
  • Turn over the top card to show a number.
    Write the number in a blank space in the top row of your game board.
  • Turn over a second and third number.
➤ Players read out the 3-digit numbers they have made.
➤ The player with the greatest number gets 1 point.
  If 2 or more players have the same number, each player gets a point.
➤ Move to the next row of your game board.

Play until one of you reaches 5 points.

Play the game again.
This time, try to make the least number.

Show *and* Share

Show how you decided where to put each number on your game board.
How did your strategy help you reach the greatest number?
The least number?

50   LESSON FOCUS | Use place value to compare and order 3-digit numbers.

Connect

➤ You can use place value to **compare** numbers.

To compare 472 and 476:

1. Compare the hundreds digits.

    4 72

    4 76

    Both have
    4 hundreds, or 400.

2. Compare the tens digits.

    4 7 2

    4 7 6

    Both have 7 tens,
    or 70.

3. Compare the ones digits.

    472

    476

    2 ones are
    less than 6 ones.

Since 2 is less than 6,
then 472 is *less than* 476   and   476 is *greater than* 472.

You can write this as:

$$472 < 476 \qquad \text{and} \qquad 476 > 472$$

This symbol means "less than."

This symbol means "greater than."

➤ You can also use place value to **order** numbers.
To order 574, 384, and 578, compare each digit.

Hundreds	Tens	Ones
5	7	4
3	8	4
5	7	8

384 has the fewest hundreds, so it is the least number.
578 and 574 have the same numbers of hundreds and tens.
574 has fewer ones than 578.
So, 574 < 578.

The order from least to greatest is 384, 574, 578.
The order from greatest to least is 578, 574, 384.

1. Which book has the greater number of stickers?
   How do you know?

   a)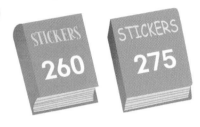

   b)

2. Copy each pair of numbers.
   Use > or < to make a true statement.
   a) 335 □ 281   **b)** 435 □ 462
   c) 705 □ 709   **d)** 162 □ 94

3. Copy each statement.
   Write a number to make each statement true.
   a) 710 > □   **b)** 984 < □
   c) 630 > □   **d)** □ < 720
   e) □ < 391   **f)** □ > 99

4. The number of dinosaurs in each box has 3 digits:
   2, 5, and 6.
   The blue box has fewer dinosaurs
   than the green box.
   How many dinosaurs could there be
   in each box?
   How do you know?
   Show your work.

5. Which is the least number? How do you know?
a) 968	**b)** 215	**c)** 158	**d)** 528
79	296	96	514
841	207	91	404
324	233	382	671

6. These numbers should be in order from least to greatest.
Find the errors. Write the numbers in the correct order.
   a) 43, 430, 417, 741
   b) 296, 207, 215, 233
   c) 404, 541, 514, 528
   d) 96, 91, 158, 149

7. Order the numbers from least to greatest.
   a) 625, 431, 662, 523
   b) 121, 99, 496, 407

8. Order the numbers from greatest to least.
   a) 510, 961, 847, 941
   b) 865, 502, 969, 45

9. Write a number between 576 and 841.
How do you know your number fits?

10. How many different 3-digit numbers can you write
with the digits 3, 4, 7?
Order the numbers from greatest to least.
How can you tell if you have found all possible numbers?

11. Look at the numbers 263 and 460.
How many digits do you need to compare
to find which number is greater? Explain.

 **Math Link**

History

Around 1900 BCE, the Babylonians counted by 60s
because there are 60 minutes in 1 hour.

Around 700 CE, the Hindus in India were counting by 10s
and using the numerals we use today.
Why do you think we count by 10s?

 Reflect

Choose 3 different numbers between 100 and 500.
Explain how to order the numbers.

Counting by 5s, 10s, 25s, and 100s

We can use a **number line** to count.

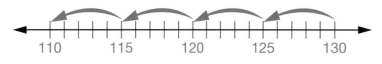

110 115 120 125 130

Start at 130. Count back by 5s.

130, 125, 120, ...

Explore

You will need a copy of blank number lines.

➤ Choose a starting number. Label it on a number line.

➤ Count on by 5s or 10s.
Record your count on the number line.

➤ Choose a different starting number. Label it.

➤ Count back by 5s or 10s. Record your count.

➤ Try different starting numbers.

Show *and* Share

Trade number lines with another pair of students.
Check each other's work.
Share the patterns that you see.

➤ To count on by 10s, start anywhere.

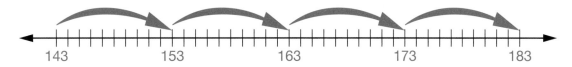

Note the pattern in the ones digits: 3, 3, 3, 3, 3, …
Think about how this would look on a hundred chart.

141	142	143	144	145	146	147	148	149	150
151	152	153	154	155	156	157	158	159	160
161	162	163	164	165	166	167	168	169	170
171	172	173	174	175	176	177	178	179	180
181	182	183	184	185	186	187	188	189	190

➤ To count back by 5s, start anywhere.

Note the pattern in the ones digits: 7, 2, 7, 2, 7, 2, …
Think about how this would look on a hundred chart.

231	232	233	234	235	236	237	238	239	240
241	242	243	244	245	246	247	248	249	250
251	252	253	254	255	256	257	258	259	260

➤ To count on or back by 100s, start anywhere.

Only the hundreds digit is changing.
It is increasing by 1 each time: 4, 5, 6, 7, 8, 9.

➤ We can also count on or back by 25s.
Start at a number that ends in 25, 50, 75, or 00.

801	802	803	804	805	806	807	808	809	810
811	812	813	814	815	816	817	818	819	820
821	822	823	824	825	826	827	828	829	830
831	832	833	834	835	836	837	838	839	840
841	842	843	844	845	846	847	848	849	850
851	852	853	854	855	856	857	858	859	860
861	862	863	864	865	866	867	868	869	870
871	872	873	874	875	876	877	878	879	880
881	882	883	884	885	886	887	888	889	890
891	892	893	894	895	896	897	898	899	900

901	902	903	904	905	906	907	908	909	910
911	912	913	914	915	916	917	918	919	920
921	922	923	924	925	926	927	928	929	930
931	932	933	934	935	936	937	938	939	940
941	942	943	944	945	946	947	948	949	950
951	952	953	954	955	956	957	958	959	960
961	962	963	964	965	966	967	968	969	970
971	972	973	974	975	976	977	978	979	980
981	982	983	984	985	986	987	988	989	990
991	992	993	994	995	996	997	998	999	1000

Start at 825. Count on:
    825, 850, 875, 900, 925, 950, 975, 1000
Note the pattern in the last 2 digits:
    25, 50, 75, 00, 25, 50, …

Start at 950. Count back:
    950, 925, 900, 875, 850, 825, …
Note the pattern in the last 2 digits:
    50, 25, 00, 75, 50, 25, …

Can you continue
my pattern?
825, 725, 625, …

1. Use number lines.
   a) Start at 129. Count on by 5s to 169.
   b) Start at 421. Count back by 10s to 321.
   c) Start at 200. Count on by 25s to 350.
   d) Start at 887. Count back by 100s to 287.

For questions 2, 3, and 4, use number lines or hundred charts.

2. Start with each number.
   Count by 5s, 10s, or 100s.
   Describe your pattern.
   a) 375   b) 812   c) 199

3. Copy each pattern. Fill in the missing numbers.
   a) □, 261, 361, 461, □   b) □, 758, 748, 738, □
   c) □, 434, 429, 424, □   d) □, 525, 550, 575, □

4. Find the mistakes in the patterns.
   Rewrite the patterns correctly.
   a) 369, 469, 669, 769   b) 876, 871, 866, 851
   c) 375, 350, 327, 300   d) 519, 509, 419, 409

5. Philippe started at 625 on
   a number line and counted on.
   He stopped at 725.
   What might his number pattern be?
   Find at least 2 ways he could
   have made the pattern.
   Show your work.

Show a number pattern of your own on a number line.
Describe the pattern.

Skip Counting with Coins

A loonie is worth one dollar.
One dollar is also 100 cents.

The coin is named after the loon, a bird
that lives in many parts of Canada.

The yellow-billed loon is
a graceful swimmer.
It dives for fish in the
Arctic wetlands.

Explore

Choose a bag of coins.
Count how much money
you have.
Record your work.

How many ways can
you find to count the money?
Use pictures, numbers,
or words to show how
you counted.

LESSON FOCUS | Use skip counting to find the value of a collection of coins.

Show *and* Share

Share your counting strategies with another pair of students.
Show them all the ways you used to count.

You can skip count to find the value of coin collections.

➤ Each quarter is worth 25 cents. Count by 25s.

25,   50,   75,   100,   125,   150,   175

The quarters are worth
one hundred seventy-five cents.
One hundred cents is one dollar.
So, we say one dollar and
seventy-five cents.

When we have more than 100 cents, we can say the amount in dollars and cents.

➤ Each dime is worth 10 cents. Count by 10s.

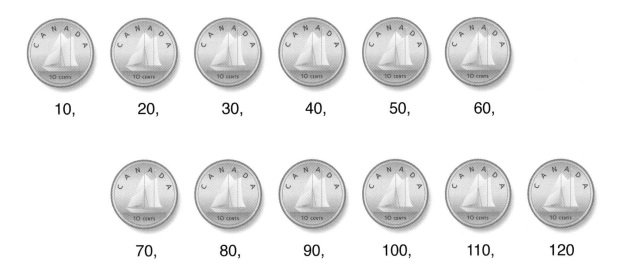

10,   20,   30,   40,   50,   60,

70,   80,   90,   100,   110,   120

The dimes are worth one hundred twenty cents.
We say one dollar and twenty cents.

Ten dimes are one dollar. So, we could also arrange the dimes like this.

one dollar

 one dollar and ten cents

 one dollar and twenty cents

The dimes are worth one dollar and twenty cents.

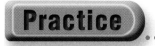

1. Draw nickels to show one dollar and five cents.

2. Count the money. Write each amount in words.

a)

b)

c)

d)

3. How much money is in each picture?

a)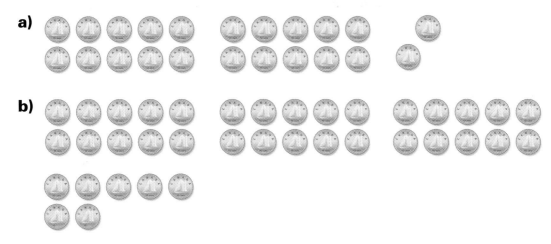

b)

c)

4. Krista counted the nickels from her bank. Is her count correct? If not, find her mistake and correct it.

> 5, 10, 15, 20, 25, 35, 40

5. David has one dollar in his pocket.
All his coins are the same.
What coins could he have?
How many solutions can you find?
How can you tell if you have found all the solutions?

Reflect

How much are twenty nickels worth?
Use pictures, words, or numbers to show your work.

Representing Numbers with Coins

Rajit has pennies, dimes, and loonies to count.

How much money does Rajit have?

Explore

You will need a tub of loonies, dimes, and pennies.
Find at least 3 ways to make two dollars.
Use pictures, numbers, or words to record the ways you find.

Show *and* Share

Share your work with another pair of students. What other ways can you find to make two dollars?

LESSON FOCUS | Represent numbers in more than one way using coins.

There are many different ways to make four dollars and fifty-two cents.

I used 4 loonies, 5 dimes, and 2 pennies.

I used 3 loonies, 15 dimes, and 2 pennies.

I used 4 loonies, 4 dimes, and 12 pennies.

1. How much money is shown in each picture?

   a)

   b)

   c)

   d)

2. Justine has two dollars and fifty cents in her pocket.
   She only has dimes, pennies, and loonies.
   What coins could she have?
   Find at least 3 solutions.

3. Use loonies, dimes, and pennies.
   Show three dollars and forty-two cents.
   Show it in as many different ways as you can.
   Use numbers, words, or pictures to show each way.

4. a) How many pennies make three dollars?
   b) How many dimes make three dollars?
   c) How many loonies make three dollars?
   Use pictures, numbers, or words to explain your thinking.

Reflect

How is using coins to represent numbers the same as using
Base Ten Blocks? How is it different?

Counting by 3s and 4s

Some things come in threes or fours.

3 Balls for $1

4 Cars for $5

How many balls are there? How many cars?

You will need copies of these charts.

1	2	3	4	5	6	7	8	9	10
11	12	13	14	15	16	17	18	19	20
21	22	23	24	25	26	27	28	29	30
31	32	33	34	35	36	37	38	39	40
41	42	43	44	45	46	47	48	49	50
51	52	53	54	55	56	57	58	59	60
61	62	63	64	65	66	67	68	69	70
71	72	73	74	75	76	77	78	79	80
81	82	83	84	85	86	87	88	89	90
91	92	93	94	95	96	97	98	99	100

101	102	103	104	105	106	107	108	109	110
111	112	113	114	115	116	117	118	119	120
121	122	123	124	125	126	127	128	129	130
131	132	133	134	135	136	137	138	139	140
141	142	143	144	145	146	147	148	149	150
151	152	153	154	155	156	157	158	159	160
161	162	163	164	165	166	167	168	169	170
171	172	173	174	175	176	177	178	179	180
181	182	183	184	185	186	187	188	189	190
191	192	193	194	195	196	197	198	199	200

Continue counting on by 3s. Colour the squares as you go.
What pattern can you find in the charts?
Record the numbers for counting by 3s.

Show *and* Share

Show your charts to a classmate.
How are your patterns the same? How are they different?
Predict the pattern for 201 to 300.

To count on by 4s, say every fourth number.

Start at 4. Count on by 4s:
　　4, 8, 12, 16, 20, 24, 28, . . .
Note the pattern in the ones digits:
　　4, 8, 2, 6, 0, 4, 8, . . .

Now start at 328.

Count back by 4s:
　　328, 324, 320, 316, 312, 308, 304, 300, 296, . . .
Note the pattern in the ones digits:
　　8, 4, 0, 6, 2, 8, 4, . . .

Practice

1. Copy each pattern and fill in the missing number.
   Describe the patterns.
   a) 9, 12, □, 18
   b) 44, 48, □, 56, □
   c) 108, 104, □, □, 92
   d) 387, □, 381, □, □

2. Use a blank number line.

    a) Start at 252. Count on by 3s to 270.

    b) Start at 69. Count back by 3s to 48.

    c) Start at 606. Count back by 3s to 582.

3. Use a blank number line.

    a) Start at 612. Count on by 4s to 640.

    b) Start at 172. Count back by 4s to 140.

    c) Start at 820. Count back by 4s to 792.

4. Find the mistakes in each pattern.
Rewrite the patterns correctly.
Describe each pattern.

    a) 186, 189, 192, 194

    b) 306, 303, 299, 297

    c) 532, 536, 540, 543

    d) 400, 396, 390, 386

5. Start at 300.
Count on or back by 3s or 4s.
Show your pattern on a number line
or a hundred chart. Describe the pattern.

6. Four rows of a hundred chart are shown.
Describe the pattern of the shaded squares.
What numbers should be shaded in the fourth row?
How do you know?

701	702	703	704	705	706	707	708	709	710
711	712	713	714	715	716	717	718	719	720
721	722	723	724	725	726	727	728	729	730
731	732	733	734	735	736	737	738	739	740

Reflect

How is counting by 3s and 4s the same as counting by 2s or 5s?
How is it different?

Estimating to 1000

Danielle is trying to figure out
how many buttons are in the jar.
How might she do this?

 **Explore** ·

Choose a bag of items.

Think about a strategy you could use to
estimate how many items are in the bag.
Work with your partner.
Make an estimate you can both agree on.
Record your estimate.

> An estimate is a thoughtful guess that is close to the number you would have if you counted all the objects.

Show and Share

Share your strategy and estimate
with another pair of students.
Count both collections.
Which estimate was closer?
Which strategy worked better?
Why do you think so?

➤ We can only see part of the sheet of paper.
Estimate how many buttons are on the whole piece of paper.

There are 10 buttons on the part we can see.
Knowing this helps us to estimate how many
buttons are on the whole paper.
This is called using 10 as a **referent**.

It looks like there is room for 3 groups
of 10 on the whole paper.
10 + 10 + 10 = 30
A thoughtful estimate is 30 buttons.

➤ Look at the 100-seed pile.
Estimate how many seeds are in the big pile.

It looks like there is room for 4 groups of 100 seeds.
100 + 100 + 100 + 100 = 400
A thoughtful estimate is 400 seeds.
We used 100 as a referent to help make an estimate.

1. Estimate how many buttons are in the big pile.
   How did you make your estimate?

10

2. Estimate how many beads are in the big bag.
   How did you make your estimate?

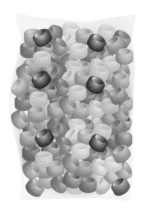 

3. Choose the best estimate for the number of blocks in
   the big pile: 313, 125, or 648.
   Explain your choice.

100

4. Do you agree or disagree with Sari's estimate? Explain your decision.

100

My estimate is 403 paper clips.

5. Which bag would be more helpful as a referent for estimating the number of pennies? Explain your choice.

6. René needs about 400 beads to complete his bookmark. How could he predict whether he has enough beads without counting all of them?

Reflect

Describe a strategy that you can use to help make a good estimate.

At Home

Look for a large collection of items. Count 10 and then make an estimate of the total number. Count 100 and make another estimate.

How Much Is 1000?

Scientists think that polar bears may be endangered because of thinning sea ice. Today, there are only about 1000 polar bears left in northeastern Manitoba.

Explore

You will need 100-grid squares and a large sheet of paper.
Arrange the 100-grid squares so their sides are touching.
Count by 100s as you add squares to your design.
Stop when you have 1000.
Glue the squares down to make a 1000 shape.

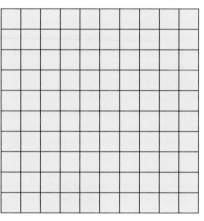

Show *and* Share

Share your work with another pair of students.
Check to see if you each have made a 1000 shape.
Explain why your work looks the same or different.
How many other 1000 shapes can you make?

Connect

Janny's stamp album has 10 pages.
Each page has 100 stamps.

How many stamps are in Janny's album?

Count by 100s:

| 100 | 200 | 300 | 400 | 500 |

| 600 | 700 | 800 | 900 | 1000 |

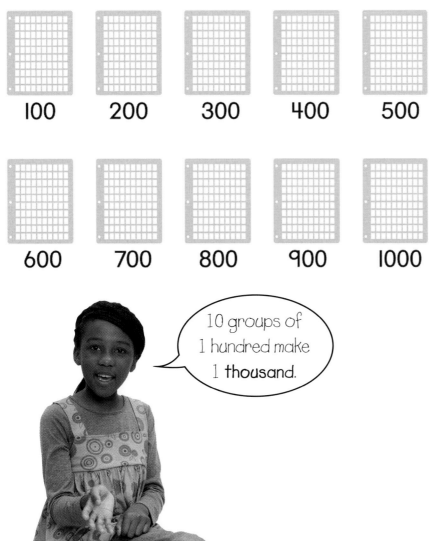

10 groups of
1 hundred make
1 thousand.

1. Are there more than 1000 or fewer than 1000:
   a) stars in the sky on a clear night?
   b) students in your school?
   c) names in a telephone book?
   d) names on a page in a telephone book?
   e) footsteps to the principal's office?

2. Are there more than 1000 or fewer than 1000 blades of grass on a lawn? How could you find out?

3. When is 1000 a big number? Explain.

4. When is 1000 a small number? Explain.

5. How could you use Base Ten Blocks to show 1000? Explain.

Reflect

When would you like to have 1000 of something? Not like to have 1000 of something? Write about your ideas.

Race to 1000

Play with up to 4 players.
You will need Base Ten Blocks and a 0 to 9 spinner.

➤ Place the Base Ten Blocks in a pile where all players can reach them.

➤ Decide who will go first.

➤ Players take turns spinning.
On your turn, collect the number of tens shown on the spinner from the pile of Base Ten Blocks.

➤ When you can, make a trade for a hundred flat or a thousand block. Trades can only be made after you draw your tens from the pile and before the next player spins.

➤ The first player who can trade for a thousand block wins.

LESSON

1   1. Show the count to find out how many.

2. Three rows of a hundred chart
are shown. Copy the rows.
Fill in the missing numbers.

491	492	493				497	498	499	
	502	503	504	505	506	507			
	512			515	516		518		520

2   3. Write the base-ten name for each number.
   a) 142   b) 891   c) 306   d) 528   e) 290

4. Explain the value of each digit in the number 444.
Use pictures, numbers, or words.

3   5. Use Base Ten Blocks to show each number 3 different ways.
Draw a picture to show each way.
   a) 154   b) 316   c) 605

5   6. Use the digits 6, 3, and 9.
   a) Make as many 3-digit numbers as you can.
   b) Order the numbers you made.
   c) Which number is the greatest? The least?

6 9   7. Use a number line.
   a) Start at 27. Count on by 5s to 62.
   b) Start at 899. Count back by 10s to 819.
   c) Start at 325. Count on by 25s to 475.
   d) Start at 220. Count on by 4s to 248.
   e) Start at 180. Count back by 3s to 150.

8. Copy each pattern. Fill in the missing numbers.
   a) □, 75, 100, 125, □   b) □, 388, 378, 368, □
   c) □, 114, 119, 124, □   d) □, 609, 606, 603, □

9. How much money is in each picture?
Record your answers in words.

a)

b)

10. Tanya has three dollars and fifty-seven cents.
She has only dimes, pennies, and loonies.
What coins could she have?

11. Choose the best estimate for the number of buttons
in the big jar: 415, 200, or 728. Explain your choice.

100

12. Are there more or fewer than 1000:
   a) people in a movie theatre?
   b) hairs on a person's head?
   c) pails of water in a lake?
Explain your thinking.

UNIT

2 Learning Goals

✓ model, compare, and order numbers to 1000

✓ explore the meaning of place value for numbers to 1000

✓ skip count by 3s, 4s, 5s, 10s, 25s, and 100s

✓ estimate a quantity using a referent

The Market

There are all kinds of exciting things to do at the market.
Many of them involve number problems.

Part 1

➤ Elisapie bought 7 wooden toys for four dollars each.
Find how much they cost.

➤ Alasie used her 100 beads as a referent to guess
the number of beads in the jar.
Do you think her guess was 487, 226, or 874? Why?

➤ Pat bought 265 cobs of corn in bags, baskets, and singles.
Show 3 ways she could have bought the corn.

➤ Justin bought a loaf of bread for three dollars.
Show 3 different ways he could have paid for the bread.

Part 2

➤ Write a story problem about the market.
➤ Solve your problem.

➤ Trade problems with a partner.
  Which problem was harder to solve for you?
  Why?

Part 3

➤ Suppose you were at the market.
  What booth would you set up?
➤ How would you use numbers
  in your booth?
  Use pictures, words, and
  numbers to show
  your ideas.

Check List

Your work should show
- ☑ how you used what you know about numbers to answer each question correctly
- ☑ how you made up and solved your story problem
- ☑ your design for a booth
- ☑ a clear explanation of your ideas

Reflect on Your Learning

Write 3 things you learned about numbers in this unit.
Use pictures, words, and numbers to explain.

3

Addition and

Plants in Our National Parks

Wildflowers, trees, and shrubs have been in Canada's National Parks for hundreds of years.

These plants have changed over time because of the actions of people or changes in the climate.

The plants provide food and shelter for birds, animals, and insects.

Learning Goals

- use strategies to recall basic addition and subtraction facts
- solve addition and subtraction equations
- estimate sums and differences for 2-digit numbers
- add and subtract 2-digit numbers mentally
- use personal strategies to add and subtract numbers with up to 3 digits
- write and solve addition and subtraction problems

Subtraction

Key Words

addition facts

doubles

near doubles

sum

related facts

subtraction facts

equation

estimate

mental math

difference

NUMBER OF PLANTS STUDIED

	TINA	MARCEL	SYLVIE	ALASIE
Week 1	8	5	6	5
Week 2	3	5	4	9
Week 3	5	7	0	1
Week 4	2	0	3	1
Total	18	17	13	16

- Who studied the most plants?

- Which weeks did someone not study any plants? How do you know?

- What else can you find out from the chart?

- Make up a question about the chart. Answer your own question.

81

Strategies for Addition Facts

What doubles fact does the ant show?

How can you use this fact to find 3 + 4 and 3 + 5?

This addition chart
is partly filled in.
What patterns do you see?

Find ways that these patterns
can help you figure out some
addition facts.

+	0	1	2	3	4	5	6	7	8	9
0	0	1								
1	1	2	3							10
2		3	4	5					10	
3			5	6	7			10		
4				7	8	9	10			
5					9	10	11			
6					10	11	12	13		
7				10			13	14	15	
8			10					15	16	17
9		10							17	18

Show *and* Share

Talk to your partner
about the addition facts
in the chart.
Record any addition strategies
you talk about.

➤ In the addition chart, the **doubles** are in the blue diagonal.
The green and pink diagonals show **near doubles**.
Near doubles are 1 more or 1 less or 2 more or 2 less than a double.

Find: 5 + 7

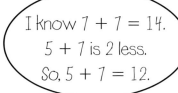

I know 5 + 5 = 10.
5 + 7 is 2 more.
So, 5 + 7 = 12.

I know 7 + 7 = 14.
5 + 7 is 2 less.
So, 5 + 7 = 12.

I took 1 from the
7 and added it to 5.
Now I have 6 + 6,
which is 12.

➤ The yellow diagonal in the addition chart shows **sums** of 10.
Making 10 or using 10 can help you figure out other facts.

Find: 8 + 6

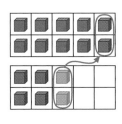

I took 2 from
the 6, leaving 4.
I added 2 to the 8 to
make 10. Then I added
the 4 to get 14.

I know 10 + 6 = 16.
8 + 6 is 2 less.
So, 8 + 6 = 14.

➤ When you add, the order does not matter.
You may find it easier to add from the larger number.

Find: 3 + 6

3 + 6 has the same sum as 6 + 3.
3 more than 6 is 9.
So, 3 + 6 = 9.

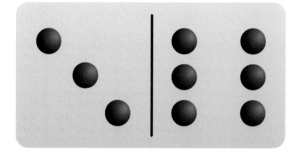

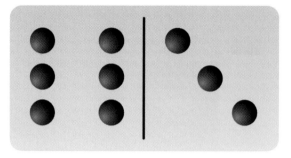

Practice

1. Think of the doubles fact 5 + 5 = 10. Find each sum.
   a) 5 + 6   **b)** 5 + 4
   c) 5 + 7   **d)** 5 + 3

2. Add. Show 2 strategies for each addition.
   a) 7 + 8   **b)** 6 + 4
   c) 9 + 8   **d)** 6 + 7

3. Add. What patterns do you see?
   a) 6 + 2   **b)** 3 + 4
       6 + 3   2 + 5
       6 + 4   1 + 6
       6 + 5   0 + 7

4. Add. How can making 10 or using 10 help you?

    a) 8 + 5   **b)** 3 + 9

    c) 9 + 6   **d)** 4 + 7

5. **a)** Add. What pattern do you notice in your answers?

       1 + 0   7 + 0

       3 + 0   9 + 0

    b) Write a rule for adding 0.

6. Add. Use any strategy you like.
Show your strategy.

    a) 7 + 9   **b)** 0 + 9

    c) 5 + 8   **d)** 4 + 8

    e) 1 + 5   **f)** 8 + 7

    g) 8 + 9   **h)** 6 + 5

7. There were 9 children in a swimming pool.
Eight more children jumped in.
How many children are in the pool?
What strategy did you use to find out?

8. Use 2 or more of these numbers each time:

      1, 2, 3, 4, 5, 6, 7, 8

Find ways to make 10.
How can you tell when you have found all the ways?
Show your work.

Reflect

What are some addition strategies you use? Use words,
pictures, or numbers to show some examples.

Relating Addition and Subtraction

Jan has 5 goldfish.

What are 2 addition facts you can write about Jan's goldfish?

Here are 2 **related facts**.

$5 - 2 = 3$ ⎤ These are **subtraction**
$5 - 3 = 2$ ⎦ **facts**.

Think about subtraction as the opposite of addition.

 **Explore**

Game

You will need about 20 blank triangle cards.

➤ Choose 2 numbers between 0 and 9. Add them.
   • On a card, write each number in a corner.
   • Write all the related facts on the other side.
➤ Continue to build your card collection.

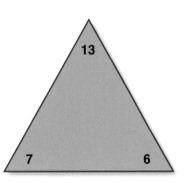

13

7   6

Show *and* Share

Share the cards to play a game. Take turns.

➤ Player 1, show the 3 numbers on the front of a card.
➤ Player 2, tell what facts are on the back of the card.
➤ You win the card when you give all the correct facts.

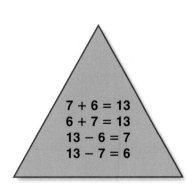

$7 + 6 = 13$
$6 + 7 = 13$
$13 - 6 = 7$
$13 - 7 = 6$

The winner is the one with the most cards at the end.

Every subtraction fact has a related addition fact.
To subtract, we can think addition.

On Monday, 13 children signed up for lacrosse.
On Tuesday, 6 more children signed up.
How many more children signed up
on Monday?

Find 13 − 6.
Think addition.
6 + ? = 13
What do I add to 6 to get 13?

> I started at 6. I need
> 4 more to get to 10,
> and 3 more to get to 13.
> 4 + 3 = 7. So, 6 + 7 = 13.

> I know 6 + 6 = 12.
> So, 6 + 7 = 13.

Since 6 + 7 = 13, then 13 − 6 = 7.

1. Write the related facts for each fact.
   a) $5 + 9 = 14$
   b) $6 + 7 = 13$
   c) $12 - 4 = 8$
   d) $14 - 7 = 7$

2. Write the related addition facts for each subtraction fact.
   a) $15 - 8 = 7$
   b) $10 - 6 = 4$
   c) $17 - 8 = 9$
   d) $11 - 5 = 6$

3. Write all the related facts that use each set of numbers.
   a) $11, 4, 7$
   b) $6, 5, 11$
   c) $9, 9, 18$
   d) $3, 9, 12$

4. Subtract. Explain your strategy.
   a) $10 - 7$
   b) $14 - 6$
   c) $18 - 9$
   d) $15 - 8$
   e) $12 - 7$
   f) $14 - 5$

5. a) Subtract. What pattern do you notice in the answers?
   $2 - 0$ $4 - 0$ $6 - 0$ $8 - 0$
   b) Write a rule for subtraction facts where one of the numbers is 0.

6. There were 17 children in line for the school bus.
   Eight children got on the bus.
   How many children were still in line?

7. Chintan read 16 books in 4 weeks.
   He read 7 books in the first 2 weeks.
   How many books did Chintan read
   in the last 2 weeks?

8. Five is one number in a subtraction fact.
   What might the other numbers be?
   Write the subtraction fact. Write all the related facts.

Reflect

How can you use addition to help you recall the answer
to a subtraction fact?

Addition and Subtraction Equations

How Many Are Missing?

You will need 18 counters. Take turns.

➤ Take between 10 and 18 counters.

➤ Put some counters in one hand and some in the other.

➤ Tell your partner how many counters you have altogether.

➤ Show how many you have in one hand.
 Ask your partner how many you have in the other hand.

Show *and* Share

What strategies did you use to find the missing number?
Share your ideas with another pair of classmates.

Connect ·

An **equation** is a statement that 2 things are equal.
These are all equations.

$7 + 3 = 10$ $8 - 3 = 5$

$10 = 7 + 3$ $5 = 8 - 3$

$2 + 8 = 7 + 3$ $10 - 5 = 8 - 3$

$7 + \square = 10$ $8 - \square = 5$

Kelsey's mother bought 15 cupcakes.
She put 6 cupcakes on a plate
and left the rest in the box.

How many cupcakes are in the box?
Use an equation to find out.

You can use a symbol to represent
the number of cupcakes in the box.

You know:

 and  makes 15 altogether

So, we can write this equation: $6 + \triangle = 15$

> You can use any symbol you like for the missing number. We use $\triangle$.

Here are some strategies children used
to solve this equation.

> Solving an equation means finding the missing number.

➤ Lisa took 15 counters.
  She put 6 of the counters in a group to show
  the number of cupcakes on the plate.
  Lisa had 9 counters left over.

  So, the missing number is 9.

➤ Abe used mental math.
  He knows $6 + 10 = 16$, so $6 + 9 = 15$.
  So, the missing number is 9.

➤ Byron used guess and check to solve $6 + \triangle = 15$.
He guessed 6 for $\triangle$ and added: $6 + 6 = 12$
The sum is too low.
He guessed 8 for $\triangle$ and added: $6 + 8 = 14$
The sum is too low, but closer to 15.
He guessed 9 for $\triangle$ and added: $6 + 9 = 15$
So, the missing number is 9.

➤ Avril started at 6 and counted up to 15.
She used a number line to keep track.

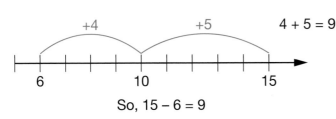

$4 + 5 = 9$

So, $15 - 6 = 9$

The missing number is 9.
There are 9 cupcakes in the box.

Practice

1. True or false?
   a) $4 + 5 = 9$
   b) $4 + 3 = 7 + 1$
   c) $5 + 2 = 3 + 4$
   d) $9 = 2 + 7$
   e) $7 + 2 = 8 + 1$
   f) $7 = 12 - 6$
   g) $3 + 1 = 10 - 6$
   h) $7 + 5 = 12 - 5$

2. Jim counted up to solve the equation
   $7 + \square = 13$.
   He used a number line to keep track.
   Solve the equation.
   How does the number line show
   the solution?

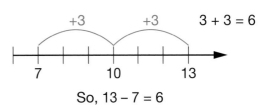

$3 + 3 = 6$

So, $13 - 7 = 6$

3. Write each equation with a different symbol.
Use counters to solve each equation. Sketch your counters.
a) $5 + \bigcirc = 14$ **b)** $\bigcirc + 3 = 11$ **c)** $5 = 5 - \bigcirc$

4. Use guess and check to solve each equation.
a) $6 + \triangle = 11$ **b)** $\bigcirc - 6 = 7$ **c)** $14 - \bigcirc = 7$

5. Solve each equation. Use any strategy you wish.
a) $12 - \square = 7$ **b)** $13 = 8 + \bigcirc$ **c)** $10 - \triangle = 8$

6. Use $+$, $-$, $=$, and $\square$, together with numbers.
Write all the equations you can for the pictures below.

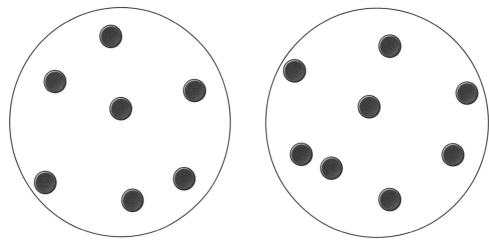

7. Sophie saw 11 lemurs at a zoo.
Seven of them were red-ruffed lemurs.
The others were ring-tailed lemurs.
How many ring-tailed lemurs
did Sophie see?
Explain your strategy.

Reflect

What is your favourite strategy for solving an addition equation?
Can you always use it?
Use words and numbers to explain.

Estimating Sums

When you do not need an exact answer, you **estimate**.
When you estimate a sum, you predict a number that is close
to the number you would get by adding.

 **Explore**

Evan's class is earning money for a charity.
They earn $46 selling tickets to a movie
and $38 at their craft sale.
About how much money did they earn?

Explain how you estimated.

Show *and* Share

Share your estimate with another pair
of classmates.
What strategies did you use?
Did you each have different answers?
Why do you think that happened?

 **Connect**

Kaori and Brian are rolling nickels their class collected for a charity.
Kaori counted 59 nickels.
Brian counted 23 nickels.
About how many nickels did they roll altogether?

Estimate to predict the sum: 59 + 23

➤ Kaori adds only the digits in the tens place.
59 has 5 tens.
23 has 2 tens.
Add the tens: 5 tens + 2 tens = 7 tens, or 70
Kaori estimates they rolled about 70 nickels.

➤ Brian takes each number to the closest 10.
59 is closest to 60.
23 is closest to 20.
Add: 60 + 20 = 80
Brian estimates they rolled about 80 nickels.

➤ Gemma takes one number to the closest 10.
59 is closest to 60.
Add: 60 + 23 = 83
Gemma estimates they rolled about 83 nickels.

There are many ways to estimate a sum.

Practice

1. Which number is the better estimate for each sum?
   a) 61 + 22 is about 80 or 90?   b) 54 + 13 is about 60 or 70?

2. Estimate each sum.
   a) 29 + 38   b) 71 + 12   c) 11 + 45   d) 44 + 44

3. Sally estimated these sums.
   Tell whether you think each estimate
   is greater than or less than the sum.
   Why do you think so?
   a) 54 + 36 is about 80
   b) 19 + 17 is about 40
   c) 27 + 62 is about 87
   d) 36 + 35 is about 70

4. Caroline's friends donated 43 stuffed animals and 26 toy cars to a toy drive.
They estimate that they donated about 70 toys.
How might they have estimated?

5. Debra has 52 stickers in her sticker book.
She was given a bag of 39 stickers.
About how many stickers does Debra have?

6. Some children chose a Canadian astronaut and a space shuttle as the topic for a project.
Forty-three chose Julie Payette on the Space Shuttle Discovery.
Thirty-eight chose Dave Williams on the Space Shuttle Endeavour.
  a) About how many worked on the projects?
  Explain 2 strategies to estimate the solution.
  b) Which strategy do you prefer? Why?

7. Thirty-two boys and 42 girls will be at a fair.
Each child will receive a prize.
Trudy and Greg want to estimate the number of prizes needed.
Trudy estimated: 30 + 40 = 70
Greg estimated: 30 + 50 = 80
  a) Show a different way to estimate the number of prizes.
  b) Which estimate would you use? Why?

Reflect

Explain the difference between guessing and estimating.
When is an estimate all that is needed?
Use examples to show your thinking.

Adding 2-Digit Numbers

Explore

Jordan's school had a Walk-A-Thon to raise money
for an animal shelter.
The teachers gave out 46 bottles of juice and 18 bottles of water.
How many drinks did the teachers give out?

➤ Estimate to predict the answer.

➤ Use any materials or strategies you wish to solve the problem.

Show *and* Share

Share your strategies with another pair of classmates.
Which strategy do you find easiest to understand?

Connect

There are 45 dogs in the animal shelter.
There are 37 cats at the same shelter.
How many cats and dogs are there in the shelter?

Find: 45 + 37

$40 + 30 = 70$.
I estimate the answer
is about 70.

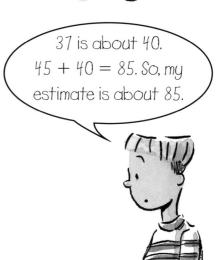

37 is about 40.
$45 + 40 = 85$. So, my
estimate is about 85.

Here are different strategies children used
to solve the problem.

➤ Hannah uses Base Ten Blocks on a place-value mat
to add 45 + 37.

Show 45 with 4 tens and 5 ones.
Show 37 with 3 tens and 7 ones.

5 ones and 7 ones is 12 ones.
Put 10 ones together to make 10.

Trade 10 ones for 1 ten.

$$\begin{array}{r} {\scriptstyle 1} \\ 45 \\ +\ 37 \\ \hline 2 \end{array}$$

This makes 8 tens and 2 ones.

$$\begin{array}{r} {\scriptstyle 1} \\ 45 \\ +\ 37 \\ \hline 82 \end{array}$$

➤ Marissa and Jeremy record 45 and 37 as tens and ones.

$45 = 40 + 5$

$37 = 30 + 7$

They add the tens and ones separately and combine the results.

- Marissa adds from left to right.
  Add the tens: $40 + 30$
  Add the ones: $5 + 7$
  Add the sums: $70 + 12$

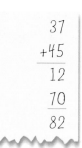

$40 + 30 = 70$
$5 + 7 = 12$
$70 + 12 = 82$

- Jeremy adds from right to left.
  Add $7 + 5$.
  Add $30 + 40$.
  Add $12 + 70$.

$$\begin{array}{r} 37 \\ +45 \\ \hline 12 \\ 70 \\ \hline 82 \end{array}$$

You can add
$37 + 45$ or $45 + 37$.

Think of other ways you can solve each problem.

There are 82 cats and dogs in the animal shelter.
The answer 82 is close to the estimates 70 and 85.

Practice

1. Estimate first. Then add.
   a) $25 + 13$ b) $11 + 67$ c) $30 + 28$ d) $44 + 34$

2. Add. Use any strategies you wish.
   a) $43 + 9$ b) $56 + 6$ c) $24 + 8$ d) $67 + 27$

3. Add. Show your strategies.

   a) $\begin{array}{r} 57 \\ + 7 \\ \hline \end{array}$ b) $\begin{array}{r} 35 \\ + 19 \\ \hline \end{array}$ c) $\begin{array}{r} 16 \\ + 78 \\ \hline \end{array}$ d) $\begin{array}{r} 28 \\ + 6 \\ \hline \end{array}$

4. Add. Record each addition sentence.

a) $50 + 35$ **b)** $49 + 34$ **c)** $48 + 33$ **d)** $47 + 32$

What patterns do you see in your answers?

5. The sum of 2 numbers is 68.
What might the numbers be?

6. Write a story problem for each addition question.

a) $63 + 28$ **b)** $54 + 9$

7. Children collected bottles to recycle.
On Monday they brought in 47 bottles.
On Tuesday they brought in 39 bottles.
How many bottles were brought in altogether?

8. For each number:
Write an addition story problem.
Estimate to predict your answer.
Solve your problem using strategies of your choice.
Use your estimate to check.

a) 35   **b)** 82

9. Make a card for each digit: 5, 3, 7, 4
Arrange the cards to make addition questions with two 2-digit numbers.

a) Find as many sums as you can.
Record each sum.

b) What is the greatest possible sum?
What is the least possible sum?
How do you know?

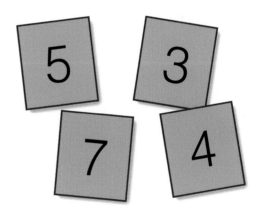

Reflect

What strategy do you prefer to use to add two 2-digit numbers?
Explain.

Using Mental Math to Add

When you add in your head, you do **mental math**.

The Toy Show has been on for 36 days.
It will be on for another 48 days.
How many days is that altogether?

Use mental math to find out.

Show *and* Share

Share your strategies with another classmate.

Connect

Here are some ways to use mental math to add.

➤ Maya adds from left to right
  to add 63 + 15.

➤ Edmond uses a "friendly"
  number to add 58 + 29.

I know 63 = 60 + 3
and 15 = 10 + 5.
60 + 10 = 70
3 + 5 = 8
70 + 8 = 78
So, 63 + 15 = 78.

60 is close to 58.
60 + 29 = 89
58 + 29 is 2 less.
So, 58 + 29 = 87.

➤ Kumail uses doubles to add 27 + 25.

I know that 25 + 25 = 50.
27 + 25 is 2 more.
So, 27 + 25 = 52.

Practice

Use mental math.

1. Add. What patterns do you see?
   a) 32 + 10   **b)** 32 + 20   **c)** 32 + 30   **d)** 32 + 40

2. Add. Use any strategies you wish.
   a) 21 + 26   **b)** 36 + 48   **c)** 45 + 15   **d)** 39 + 27

3. Add.
   a) 35 + 29   **b)** 48 + 18   **c)** 23 + 67   **d)** 16 + 55

4. How many different ways can you find 29 + 55?
   Use words, pictures, or numbers to show each way.

5. Josh and Kara were counting licence plates.
   Josh counted 49 plates from Alberta.
   Kara counted 33 plates from Manitoba.
   How many licence plates did they count?
   Use words, pictures, or numbers to explain your strategy.

Reflect

Describe 2 strategies you could use to
add 48 + 24 in your head.

Adding 3-Digit Numbers

Explore

St. Mark's School sells T-shirts for gym classes.
236 children ordered blue T-shirts.
175 children ordered red T-shirts.

How many T-shirts were ordered?
Use materials or strategies of your choice
to solve this problem.

Show *and* Share

Show how you found the total number of T-shirts.
Share your strategy with another pair of classmates.
Try the strategy of another pair to add two 3-digit numbers.

Connect

St. Mark's School also sells hats.
It sold 257 blue hats and 165 white hats.
How many hats were sold altogether?

Find: 257 + 165

$200 + 100 = 300$
The answer will be
more than 300.

$300 + 200 = 500$
The answer will be less
than 500.

➤ Ross uses Base Ten Blocks on a place-value mat to add 257 + 165.

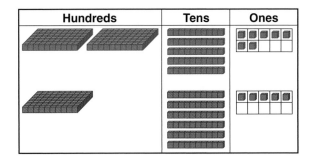

Show 257 with
2 hundreds, 5 tens, and 7 ones.
Show 165 with
1 hundred, 6 tens, and 5 ones.

$$\begin{array}{r} 257 \\ + \; 165 \\ \hline \end{array}$$

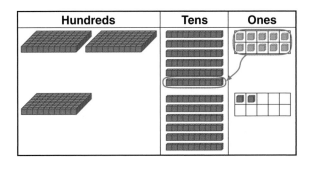

Add the ones:
7 ones + 5 ones = 12 ones
Put 10 ones together to make 10.

Regroup 10 ones as 1 ten.

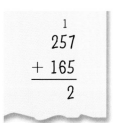

$$\begin{array}{r} {}^{1} \\ 257 \\ + \; 165 \\ \hline 2 \end{array}$$

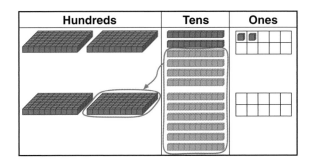

Add the tens:
1 ten + 5 tens + 6 tens = 12 tens
Regroup 10 tens as 1 hundred.
That's 4 hundreds, 2 tens, and 2 ones.

$$\begin{array}{r} {}^{1\,1} \\ 257 \\ + \; 165 \\ \hline 422 \end{array}$$

➤ Jas and Nadia think of 165 as 100 + 60 + 5.
They think of 257 as 200 + 50 + 7.

• Jas uses the order 165 + 257 and adds from left to right.

$$100 + 200 = 300$$
$$60 + 50 = 110$$
$$5 + 7 = 12$$
$$300 + 110 = 410$$
$$410 + 12 = 422$$

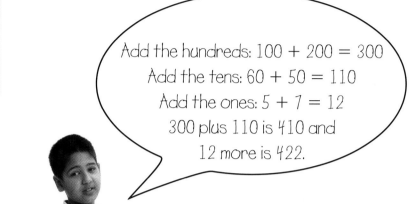

Add the hundreds: $100 + 200 = 300$
Add the tens: $60 + 50 = 110$
Add the ones: $5 + 7 = 12$
300 plus 110 is 410 and
12 more is 422.

• Nadia uses the order 257 + 165 and adds from right to left.

$$7 + 5 = 12$$
$$50 + 60 = 110$$
$$12 + 110 = 122$$
$$200 + 100 = 300$$
$$300 + 122 = 422$$

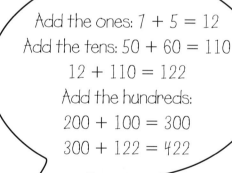

Add the ones: $7 + 5 = 12$
Add the tens: $50 + 60 = 110$
$12 + 110 = 122$
Add the hundreds:
$200 + 100 = 300$
$300 + 122 = 422$

There are 422 hats.

Think of other ways
to solve the problem.

1. Add.
   a) 290 + 61
   b) 9 + 479
   c) 502 + 349
   d) 177 + 674

2. Use any strategy to find the sum.
   a)   340
      + 270

   b)   71
      + 459

   c)   382
      + 8

   d)   293
      + 237

3. A family reunion was held in a park.
   There were 137 children and 218 adults.
   How many lunches were needed
   for the people at the reunion?

4. Write a story problem that can be solved
   by adding two 3-digit numbers.
   Solve the problem.
   Explain your solution.

5. The sum of 2 numbers is 624.
   What might the numbers be for each of these?
   a) One number has 1 digit.
      The other number has 3 digits.
   b) One number has 2 digits.
      The other number has 3 digits.
   c) Each number has 3 digits.

6. Add. What patterns do you see in the answers?
   Explain the patterns.
   a)   4 + 5
       40 + 50
      400 + 500

   b) 400 + 213
      400 + 313
      400 + 413
      400 + 513

Reflect

How is adding two 3-digit numbers like adding
two 2-digit numbers? How is it different? Explain.

Tic Tac Add

You will need a *Tic Tac Add* game board, 1 red Snap Cube, 1 yellow Snap Cube, 18 red counters, and 18 yellow counters.

The object of the game is to get 3 counters in a row.

➤ Player A puts a red Snap Cube on any number in the Player A row.

➤ Player B puts a yellow Snap Cube on any number in the Player B row.

➤ Player B adds the numbers under the Snap Cubes.
Player A adds to check.
Player B puts a yellow counter over the sum
on the game board.

Use any strategy you wish.

➤ Player A moves the red Snap Cube
to a different number in the Player A row.

➤ Player A adds the numbers under the Snap Cubes.
Player B adds to check.
Player A puts a red counter over the sum on the game board.

➤ You may only put 1 counter over a number on the game board.
Continue taking turns until someone gets 3 in a row.

Estimating Differences

When you estimate a **difference**, you predict a number
that is close to the number you would get by subtracting.

Explore

Calaway Park is in Calgary, Alberta.
It has a ride called the Dream Machine
that can take 56 passengers.
Thirty-three people are on the ride.

How many more people
can get on the ride?

Estimate to predict a number
that is close to the answer.
Record how you estimate.

Show *and* Share

Share estimates and strategies
with another pair of classmates.
Are the estimates different for
different strategies?

Connect

Marla had 87¢.
She spent some of her money.
She has 34¢ left.
About how much did Marla spend?

Estimate to predict the difference: 87 − 34

Here are different strategies children used to estimate.

➤ Jill writes each number to the closest 10.
87 is closest to 90.
34 is closest to 30.
Subtract: 90 − 30 = 60
Jill estimates that Marla spent about 60¢.

➤ Robert subtracts only the digits in the tens place.
87 has 8 tens.
34 has 3 tens.
Subtract the tens: 8 tens − 3 tens = 5 tens, or 50
Robert estimates that Marla spent about 50¢.

➤ Max uses the number of tens for the number he subtracts.
34 has 3 tens.
Subtract 3 tens: 87 − 30 = 57
Max estimates that Marla spent about 57¢.

Think of other estimation strategies.

Practice

1. Estimate each difference.
   a) 64 − 35   b) 87 − 68
   c) 34 − 15   d) 75 − 55
   e) 53 − 40   f) 91 − 29

2. Tell how Al might have estimated each difference.
   a) 52 − 24 is about 32   b) 84 − 58 is about 30
   c) 79 − 17 is about 60   d) 63 − 36 is about 20

3. Choose one part in question 2.
   Show another way to estimate the difference.

4. The Yukon Arctic Wolves soccer team won 3 out of 5 games at the national championships in 2007. They had 92 people watching their game against Saskatchewan. Fifty-nine of the people took pictures.
   About how many people did not take pictures?

5. Jerome had a package of 85 balloons.
He used 57 balloons for a party.
He estimates that he has about 30 balloons left.

   a) How might Jerome have estimated?

   b) Use a different strategy to estimate the number of balloons Jerome has left.
   Compare your estimate with Jerome's.

6. Faizal had 136 marbles. He gave away 25.
Faizal says he now has about 80 marbles.
Do you agree? Why or why not?

7. Heidi went to Calaway Park.
She counted the people in line for the Flying Ace.
She counted the people in line for the Ocean Motion.
Heidi estimated the difference was about 10 people.
How many people might be in each line?
Use words, pictures, or numbers to explain your thinking.

At Home

Reflect

Strategies for estimating differences can give different estimates. Sometimes the estimates are the same.
Use examples to show this.

Next time you go shopping, find a way to estimate a sum or difference.

Subtracting 2-Digit Numbers

Explore

Baby salmon are called fry.
There were 74 fry swimming in a stream.
Forty-seven of them swam into the ocean.
How many fry didn't swim into the ocean?

➤ First, estimate to predict the answer.

➤ Then use any materials or strategies
you wish to solve the problem.

➤ Use your estimate to check your solution.

Show *and* Share

Share your answers and strategies with another
pair of classmates.

Connect

Some children were given the
numbers 45 and 16 to create
a subtraction problem.
They created this problem.

Carlo's farm has 45 horses.
Sixteen of the horses are colts.
How many of the horses are not colts?

For 45 − 16, I'll estimate
the answer as 40 − 10,
or 30.

Here are different strategies children used to
subtract 45 − 16.

➤ Cory uses Base Ten Blocks
   on a place value mat.

45
− 16

I can split 45 into
30 + 15, which is
3 tens and 15 ones.

minus [1] [6]

I take away 6 ones
and 1 ten.

I have 2 tens
and 9 ones left.
That's 29.

➤ Paul counts on from 16 to 45.

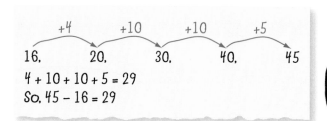

$4 + 10 + 10 + 5 = 29$
So, $45 - 16 = 29$

I think addition.
I count on.

➤ Petra subtracts by skip counting backward.

I think of 16 as
10 and 5 and 1.

Start at 45.
Subtract 10, then 5, then 1.
45 … 35 … 30 … 29

$45 - 10 = 35$
$35 - 5 = 30$
$30 - 1 = 29$
So, $45 - 16 = 29$

There are 29 horses that are not colts.
The answer is close to the estimate of 30.

Practice

1. Estimate. Which answers will be more than 20?
   Subtract if the estimate is less than 20.
   a) $58 - 24$ **b)** $39 - 25$ **c)** $57 - 23$ **d)** $66 - 22$

2. Use any strategy you wish to find each difference.
   Show your strategy.
   a) $35 - 9$ **b)** $74 - 48$ **c)** $43 - 7$ **d)** $82 - 76$

3. Subtract.
   a) $\begin{array}{r} 47 \\ -\ 20 \\ \hline \end{array}$ **b)** $\begin{array}{r} 56 \\ -\ 29 \\ \hline \end{array}$ **c)** $\begin{array}{r} 50 \\ -\ 9 \\ \hline \end{array}$ **d)** $\begin{array}{r} 89 \\ -\ 62 \\ \hline \end{array}$

4. Subtract.

91 − 56

91 − 66

91 − 76

91 − 86

What patterns do you see in your answers?

5. There were 16 girls in the gym. After the boys arrived, there were 25 children in the gym.
How many boys came into the gym?

6. A Grade 3 class had a family movie night.
They counted 73 students and 56 parents.
Were there more students or more parents? How many more?
Estimate first, then calculate.
Use your estimate to check your answer.

7. The difference of two 2-digit numbers is 35.

a) What might the numbers be?
Find 4 answers.
Write the subtraction equation for each answer.
What strategy did you use to find the answers?

b) Choose a subtraction from part a.
Create a story problem to match it.

Reflect

Suppose a friend missed school today.
Use words, pictures, or numbers to explain to your friend how to subtract two 2-digit numbers.

Using Mental Math to Subtract

 **Explore**

There were 43 people skating.
Twenty-seven people left.
How many people are still skating?

Use mental math to find out.

Show *and* Share

Share your strategies with another pair of classmates.

Connect

Here are some ways to use mental math to subtract.

➤ Ross uses a "friendly" number to subtract 73 − 49.

➤ Bonnie finds 85 − 56 by counting up from 56 to 85.

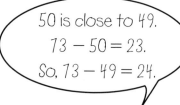

50 is close to 49.
73 − 50 = 23.
So, 73 − 49 = 24.

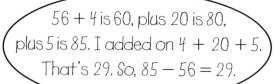

56 + 4 is 60, plus 20 is 80,
plus 5 is 85. I added on 4 + 20 + 5.
That's 29. So, 85 − 56 = 29.

➤ Olivia thinks of addition and uses doubles to subtract 22 − 11.

I know 11 + 11 = 22.
So, 22 − 11 = 11.

➤ Lars matches the ones to subtract 64 − 38.

I can add 4 to 64
to get 68.
68 - 38 = 30
Then, I take away
the 4 I added.
30 - 4 = 26
So, 64 - 38 = 26

Practice

Use mental math.

1. Subtract. What patterns do you see?
   a) 63 − 41   **b)** 73 − 31   **c)** 83 − 21   **d)** 93 − 11

2. Subtract. Show your strategies.
   a) 87 − 78   **b)** 53 − 49   **c)** 35 − 27   **d)** 72 − 69

3. Subtract.
   a) 74 − 56   **b)** 92 − 18   **c)** 67 − 35   **d)** 85 − 47

4. What different ways can you use mental math to find 81 − 58?
   Use words, pictures, or numbers to show each way.

5. There were 32 geese on a beach. More geese flew in. Then there were 61 geese. How many geese flew in?

6. The answer is 43. What could the subtraction problem be?

Reflect

Explain 2 mental math strategies you can use to subtract.

Subtracting 3-Digit Numbers

There are 282 beads in the jar.
Robert estimated 300.
Brenda estimated 269.

Whose estimate was closer? How much closer?

Show and Share

Share your solution with another pair of classmates.
What strategies did you use?

Connect

Sundin and Bonita had a ball bouncing contest.
Sundin bounced a ball 402 times.
Bonita bounced a ball 128 times.
How many more times did Sundin bounce a ball?

Find: 402 − 128

➤ Tasia counts up from 128 to 402.

```
      +2      +70     +200      +2
128,     130,     200,     400,     402
2 + 70 + 200 + 2 = 274
So, 402 − 128 = 274
```

I count up. I write the numbers, then add them.

➤ Joe uses Base Ten Blocks on a place-value mat to subtract.

$$\begin{array}{r} 402 \\ -\ 128 \\ \hline \end{array}$$

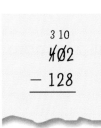

I can split 402 into 300 + 100 + 2, which is 3 hundreds, 10 tens, and 2 ones.

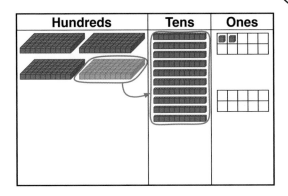

... I need more ones. I trade 1 ten for 10 ones. So, I have 3 hundreds, 9 tens, and 12 ones.

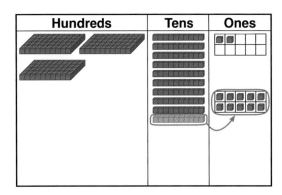

... I take away 1 hundred, 2 tens, and 8 ones. That leaves 2 hundreds, 7 tens, and 4 ones. That's 274.

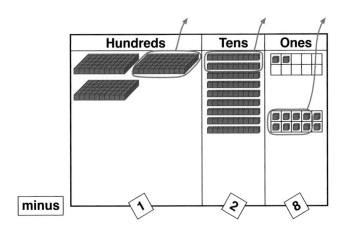

➤ Tom counts backward to subtract 402 − 128.

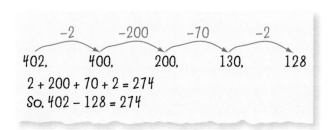

$2 + 200 + 70 + 2 = 274$
So, $402 - 128 = 274$

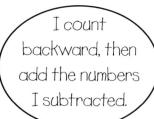

I count backward, then add the numbers I subtracted.

Sundin bounced a ball 274 more times.

Practice

1. Subtract.

a)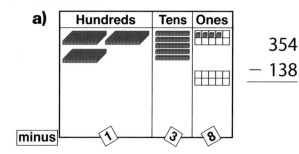

$$354 - 138$$

b)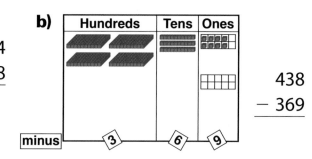

$$438 - 369$$

2. Subtract. Explain your strategies.
   a) $876 - 9$ b) $923 - 10$ c) $635 - 22$ d) $599 - 86$

3. Subtract.
   a) $756 - 49$ b) $830 - 7$ c) $687 - 39$ d) $940 - 35$

4. Subtract.
   a) $483 - 156$ b) $557 - 230$ c) $654 - 327$ d) $701 - 374$

5. Subtract.

a) 200
    − 82

b) 300
    − 183

c) 400
    − 284

d) 500
    − 285

6. Jenna subtracted 785 − 575 like this.

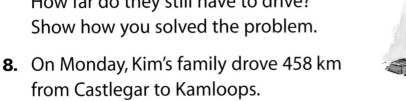

700 − 500 = 200
80 − 70 = 10
5 − 5 = 0

a) Finish Jenna's subtraction.
Explain her strategy.

b) Use a different strategy to subtract the same numbers.

c) Compare the strategies in parts a and b.
Which strategy do you prefer? Why?

7. A campground is 475 km from the Kapurs' home.
Before lunch the Kapurs drove 238 km.
How far do they still have to drive?
Show how you solved the problem.

8. On Monday, Kim's family drove 458 km
from Castlegar to Kamloops.
On Tuesday, they drove from Kamloops
to Merritt.
They drove a total of 544 km over the 2 days.
How many kilometres did they drive on Tuesday?
Write an equation to solve the problem.
Solve the equation.
Answer the question in the problem.

9. Write a story problem that can be
solved using 652 − 328.
Solve the problem. Explain your strategy.

Reflect

What strategy would you use to find 300 − 157?
Use pictures, numbers, or words to explain.

12

Solving Addition and Subtraction Problems

Explore

Lu-Anne and Fisher helped clean up in the gym.
Lu-Anne picked up 243 bean bags.
Fisher picked up 206 bean bags.

➤ Make an addition problem and a subtraction problem about picking up the bean bags.

➤ Solve your problems.

Show and Share

Share your problems and solutions with another pair of classmates. How did you know whether to add or subtract?

Connect

Sometimes you need to decide whether to add or subtract when you solve a problem.

One year, it rained on 148 days in Victoria, British Columbia.
The next year, it rained on 163 days in Victoria.

➤ On how many days did it rain during these 2 years?

Jason added to solve the problem.
He thought of 148 as 100 + 40 + 8 and 163 as 100 + 60 + 3.
He then added from left to right.

$148 = 100 + 40 + 8$
$163 = 100 + 60 + 3$
$100 + 100 = 200$
$40 + 60 = 100$
$8 + 3 = 11$
$200 + 100 + 11 = 311$

There are many strategies Jason could use.

It rained on 311 days during these 2 years.

➤ How many more days did it rain in the second year?

Jody subtracted to solve the problem.
She thought of 163 as 150 + 13.
To find 163 − 148, Jody subtracted 148
from 150 + 13.

$163 = 150 + 13$
$150 - 148 = 2$
$2 + 13 = 15$

So, 163 − 148 = 15.

It rained 15 more days during the
second year.

I wrote 163 as 150 + 13 because it is easy to subtract 148 from 150.

1. Find each missing number. What patterns can you see?
   a) $174 = 169 + \square$
      $174 = 164 + \square$
      $174 = 159 + \square$
   b) $658 = 600 + \square$
      $658 = 590 + \square$
      $658 = 580 + \square$
   c) $809 = 810 - \square$
      $809 = 820 - \square$
      $809 = 830 - \square$

2. a) The difference between two 3-digit numbers is 246.
      What might the numbers be? Give 3 possible answers.
   b) The sum of two 3-digit numbers is 246.
      What might the numbers be? Give 3 possible answers.

3. Each sentence below is an answer to a story problem.
   Write 1 addition story or 1 subtraction story for each sentence.
   a) Boyle, Alberta, has 840 people.
   b) There are 194 whooping cranes in the Wood Buffalo flock
      of the Northwest Territories.
   c) A year has 365 days.

4. A Grade 3 class in Saskatoon planted tulips.
   They planted 256 red tulips and 371 yellow tulips.
   a) How many more yellow tulips than red tulips did they plant?
   b) How many tulips did they plant altogether?
   Explain how you solved these problems.

5. Grade 2 and Grade 3 children rode on a bus to a museum.
   There were 19 Grade 2 children.
   There were 25 Grade 3 children.
   How many children were on the bus?

6. Prya and Jody collected donations for the Terry Fox Run.
Prya collected $82.
Jody collected $129.

   a) Who collected more money?
   How much more did she collect?

   b) Did you add or subtract? Explain.

7. A school in Whitehorse was collecting things to recycle.
Children brought in 277 cans and 95 bottles.
How many things did they bring?

8. Zane, Sunny, and Michelle are playing video games.
Zane's score is 456. Sunny's score is 285.
Michelle's score is 369.

   a) How many points does Sunny need to tie Michelle?

   b) How many points do Michelle and Sunny each need to tie Zane?

   c) Make up your own problem about these scores.
   Solve your problem.

9. Write a story problem that can be solved by adding or subtracting two 3-digit numbers. Solve the problem.

Math Link

Some places have snow on the ground for most of the year. How many days in a year does each place not have snow on the ground?

Place	Number of Days
Alert, Nunavut	306
High Level, Alberta	212
Whitehorse, Yukon	165

Reflect

Describe a strategy for adding or subtracting 3-digit numbers.
Explain your strategy to a classmate.

Strategies Toolkit

Explore

Savannah, Ken, and April made friendship bracelets.

Savannah used 3 fewer beads than Ken.
Ken used 2 more beads than April.
April used 22 beads. Five beads are left.
How many beads were in the bag?

Show and Share

Explain how you solved the problem.

Connect

It's Jump Rope for Heart Day!

Bessie jumped 9 fewer times than Francis.
Francis jumped 12 more times than Henry.
Henry jumped 52 times.
What was their total number of jumps?
Here is one way to solve this problem.

Strategies

- **Make a chart.**
- **Use a model.**
- **Draw a picture.**
- **Solve a simpler problem.**
- **Work backward.**
- **Guess and test.**
- **Make an organized list.**
- **Use a pattern.**

What do you know?
- Henry jumped 52 times.
- Francis jumped 12 more times than Henry.
- Bessie jumped 9 fewer times than Francis.

Think of a strategy to help you solve the problem.
- You can **work backward**.
  Start with the number of times Henry jumped.

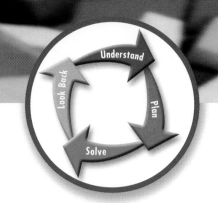

- How many times did Henry jump?
- How many times did Francis jump?
- How many times did Bessie jump?
- How many times did they jump altogether?

How do you know your answer is correct?
How could you solve this problem another way?

Practice

Choose one of the
Strategies

1. Kumail and Sasha are playing a game.
   Kumail has won 7 cards.
   Sasha has won 6 more cards than Kumail.
   There are 24 cards left.
   How many cards are there altogether?

2. Margaret uses nickels and dimes to buy
   a bookmark.
   It costs 65¢. Margaret paid with 8 coins.
   How many of each coin did she use?

3. At a garage sale, there are bicycles and
   tricycles. Altogether, there are 18 wheels.
   How many bicycles and tricycles are there?

Reflect

Think about one of these problems you solved.
Use words, pictures, or numbers to explain how you solved it.

LESSON

1
2

1. Add or subtract. Show your strategies.
   a) 5 + 9   b) 17 − 8   c) 6 + 8   d) 18 − 9

2. Mia has 2 number cubes.
   Each number cube has the numbers
   0, 4, 5, 6, 7, and 8.
   a) Mia rolls both number cubes and
      adds the numbers.
      What sums might Mia get?
   b) What differences might Mia get
      if she subtracts the numbers rolled?

3. A lacrosse team has 16 players.
   Nine of them are girls.
   How many of the players are boys?

3

4. Find each missing number.
   a) 6 + □ = 15   b) □ + 7 = 14
   c) 17 − □ = 9   d) □ − 8 = 7

5. The library had 12 books about the moon.
   Penny borrowed some of them.
   There are 4 books left.
   Write and solve an equation to find
   how many books Penny borrowed.

4
8

6. Estimate each sum or difference. Explain your strategies.
   a) 42 + 29   b) 53 − 17   c) 23 + 28   d) 85 − 49

4
5
8
9

7. Estimate. Then add or subtract.
   a) 67 + 18   b) 72 − 69   c) 14 + 79   d) 53 − 28

5
7

8. Add.
   a)   25   b)   247   c)   156   d)   349
      + 36   + 19   + 232   + 267

6
10

9. Use mental math to add or subtract.
   a) 31 + 32   **b)** 97 − 35   **c)** 64 − 26   **d)** 75 + 19

10. Explain how to use mental math to solve.
   a) 38 + 45   **b)** 50 − 18

7

11. The classroom floor was retiled.
    It needed 476 red tiles and 385 yellow tiles.
    How many tiles were needed altogether?

9
11

12. Subtract.

a)	**b)**	**c)**	**d)**
78	690	385	500
− 23	− 52	− 256	− 187

11

13. There were 750 children at summer camp.
    After 1 week, 252 children went home.
    How many children were left at the camp?

12

14. Jenny jumped 124 times on the
    trampoline. Shane jumped 73 times
    on the trampoline.
    a) How many times did they jump
       altogether?
    b) How many more times did Jenny
       jump than Shane?

15. Use numbers with 1, 2, or 3 digits.
    Write an addition and a subtraction
    equation with each answer.
    a) 326   **b)** 307
    c) 608   **d)** 281

16. Use 3-digit numbers. Create a story
    problem with the answer 376.

U N I T

3 Learning Goals

☑ use strategies to recall
   basic addition and
   subtraction facts

☑ solve addition and
   subtraction equations

☑ estimate sums and
   differences for 2-digit
   numbers

☑ add and subtract 2-digit
   numbers mentally

☑ use personal strategies to
   add and subtract numbers
   with up to 3 digits

☑ write and solve addition
   and subtraction problems

Plants in Our National Parks

Native plants have been growing
in national parks for hundreds of years.

NATIVE PLANTS IN NATIONAL PARKS

NATIONAL PARK	NUMBER OF TYPES OF PLANTS
Yoho, British Columbia	587
Ivvavik, Yukon	242
Banff, Alberta	846
Aulavik, Northwest Territories	154
Quttinirpaaq, Nunavut	134
Prince Albert, Saskatchewan	564
Riding Mountain, Manitoba	623

Source: Parks Canada, 2005

National parks also have plants that are not
native to the parks.

NON-NATIVE PLANTS IN NATIONAL PARKS

NATIONAL PARK	NUMBER OF TYPES OF PLANTS
Yoho, British Columbia	58
Banff, Alberta	77
Aulavik, Northwest Territories	3
Prince Albert, Saskatchewan	88

Source: Parks Canada, 2005

Use the information in the charts.
Use words, numbers, and equations to show your thinking.

Part 1
Aulavik means "a place where people travel."
➤ For travellers at Aulavik, how many different types of plants might they see?

➤ Which park has more native plant types, Riding Mountain or Yoho?
How many more?

Part 2
A botanist is a scientist who studies plants.
➤ Suppose a botanist discovered 35 more native types of plants in each park.
How many native plant types would be in each park then?
Make a chart to show your answers.

Part 3
➤ Choose a park from the second chart.
Use any information you have about that park.
Write an addition or subtraction story problem.
Solve your problem.

Check List
Your work should show
- ☑ how you estimate, add, and subtract to find sums and differences
- ☑ that you can decide whether to add or subtract
- ☑ how you made up and solved your story problem
- ☑ a clear explanation of your work and ideas

Reflect on Your Learning

What are some important things you know about adding and subtracting?
Give at least 2 examples in your explanation.

UNIT

1

1. Which picture extends this pattern?
Explain why you think so.

a)   **b)**

2. **a)** Use grid paper. Make a pattern that starts with 2 ⬜s, and adds 2 ⬜s each time.

   b) Make a different pattern that starts with 2 ⬜s, and adds 4 ⬜s each time.

   c) How are your patterns the same? Different?

3. What is the pattern rule?
Copy the pattern to fill in the missing numbers.
   a) 36, 38, __, __, 44, 46, __   **b)** 22, 32, __, 52, __, __, 82

4. Use grid paper.
   a) Make a decreasing pattern.
   Show the first 4 figures.
   b) Write your pattern rule.

2

5. Draw a picture to show each number.
Then record the number in a place-value chart.
   a) 75   **b)** 249   **c)** 503   **d)** 230

6. Copy each pair of numbers.
Use < or > to make each statement true.
   a) 73 ⬜ 730   **b)** 874 ⬜ 851
   c) 934 ⬜ 936   **d)** 208 ⬜ 199

7. Tim, PJ, and Carey have card collections.
   Tim has 124 cards. PJ has 205 cards.
   Carey has more cards than Tim, but fewer than PJ.
   How many cards might Carey have?

8. Record your count each time.
   a) Start at 137. Count on by 5s to 172.
   b) Start at 972. Count back by 10s to 852.
   c) Start at 234. Count on by 4s to 254.

9. Jamie started at 738. She started to count back by 5s.
   Would she ever reach 635? Explain why you think so.

10. Maya has pennies, dimes, and loonies.
    She has four dollars and thirty-seven cents altogether.
    Show 3 different ways she could have that much money.

11. Find each missing number. Explain your strategy.
    a) $9 + \square = 12$ **b)** $18 - \square = 9$ **c)** $\square + 5 = 13$

12. Add or subtract.
    a) $368 + 292$ **b)** $409 + 567$ **c)** $734 - 576$
    d) $801 - 699$ **e)** $310 + 259$ **f)** $499 - 218$

13. A shopkeeper had 738 balloons. She sold 579.
    How many were left? Explain your strategy.

14. A school planted trees in the park.
    The students planted 183 pine trees and 231 cedar trees.
    a) How many more cedar trees than pine trees did they plant?
    b) How many of both type of tree did they plant?

15. The answer is 427.
    What could the question be?
    Write a story problem that will give the answer 427.

Measurement

4

Eat Your Veggies

Learning Goals

- use non-standard and standard units to measure the passage of time
- use a calendar
- measure length, width, and height in centimetres and in metres
- measure perimeter in centimetres and in metres
- measure the mass of an object in grams and in kilograms

Key Words

· · · · · · · · · · · · · · · · · · · ·

unit

hour (h)

minute (min)

second (s)

calendar

length

width

height

centimetre (cm)

metre (m)

referent

perimeter

mass

kilogram (kg)

gram (g)

Yoko and Sandar like to grow their own vegetables. They care for their garden all summer.

How could they measure the length of a carrot? The height of a corn stalk? The distance around a garden?

How else could they measure?

133

Measuring the Passage of Time

Which takes more time?
• tying your shoes
• getting dressed to go out in the snow
Which takes less time?
• making bannock
• eating a piece of bannock
How could you find out?

Explore

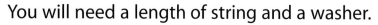

You will need a length of string and a washer.

➤ Make a pendulum timer.
Practise making
the pendulum swing as you
count the swings.

➤ Use your pendulum.
Measure how long it takes your
partner to do each activity.
• say the alphabet
• draw 10 happy faces
• print your name 5 times
• do an activity of your choice
Record your work.

Activity	Number of Swings
say the alphabet	
draw 10 happy faces	

Show *and* Share

Which activity took the most time? The least time?
How do you know?
Compare your results with another pair of classmates.
Why might your results be different?

Connect

· ·

We can measure how much time an activity takes using different units.

It takes Sam 15 pendulum
swings to do up his mukluks.

It takes 1 song on the
radio to get to the store.

It takes Hana 1 TV show
to brush her dog.

It takes 2 recesses
to build a snow fort.

Practice

· ·

Work with a partner for questions 1 to 3. Use your pendulum timers.

1. Measure how long it takes to do the activity.
    a) counting by 5s to 50
    b) drawing a snowman
    c) taking off your shoes and putting them on again
    d) writing the numbers 1 to 30

2. Find an activity that takes about 25 pendulum swings.
Record your activity in pictures or words.

3. Which activity takes more time?
   a) clapping 6 times or counting to 20
   b) drawing a clown face or hopping 10 times
   c) finding page 237 in your math book or saying the alphabet

4. Which unit would you use to measure the time it takes for each activity? Explain each choice.

   a) going to the library
      • pendulum swings or TV shows?
   b) brushing your hair
      • TV commercials or TV shows?
   c) singing "O Canada"
      • pendulum swings or recesses?
   d) putting on snowshoes
      • TV shows or pendulum swings?

5. Choose the better estimate.
   a) doing your homework
      • 1 TV show or 5 TV shows?
   b) playing a board game
      • 1 recess or 3 recesses?
   c) making your bed
      • 1 TV commercial or 4 TV commercials?

6. Name 2 ways that you measure how long an activity takes.

At Home

Reflect

Explain how you choose which unit to use to measure how much time it takes to do an activity.

Choose an activity you do at home. What unit could you use to measure how long it takes? Estimate how long you think it will take, then check.

Exploring Units of Time

About how long is a minute? The red hand goes around the clock once in one **minute**. It goes from one mark to the next in one **second**.

Just a minute.

 **Explore** •

You will need a clock or a watch with a second hand.
Take turns to time your partner.

➤ What can you do in one minute?
  • How high can you count by ones?
  • How many hearts can you draw?
  • How many times can you tie a shoe?

Activity	Kim	Kerri
Counting	123	108
Drawing hearts	59	
Tying a shoe		

➤ What can you do in one second?
  • Can you print your name?
  • Can you blink twice?
  • Can you touch your toes 5 times?

Show *and* Share

Share your results with another pair of students.
Are they the same or different?
Why do you think that is?

Connect

Time is measured in different units.

The **minute** (min) is a short unit of time.
It takes one minute (1 min) for the **minute hand** to
move from one mark on the clock to the next.

It takes about 1 min
to brush your teeth.

It takes about 5 min
to fill a bathtub.

It takes about 15 min
to eat lunch.

The **hour** (h) is a longer unit of time. It takes one hour
(1 h) for the **hour hand** to move from one number on the clock
to the next.

My soccer game
takes about an hour.

Children should get about
10 h of sleep each night.

The **second** (s) is a very short unit of time.
It takes one second (1 s) for the **second hand** to
move from one mark on the clock to the next.

It takes 1 s to say
"One second."

It takes about 10 s to
button my shirt.

Here are ways that some units of time are related.
One minute = sixty seconds (1 min = 60 s)
One hour = sixty minutes (1 h = 60 min)

Practice

1. Would you use minutes or hours to measure how long it takes to
   a) make a sandwich?
   b) read a chapter book?
   c) build a birdhouse?
   d) take a shower?

2. Choose the better estimate.
   a) Drink a glass of milk.
   • 5 min or 45 min?
   b) Count to 100.
   • 1 min or 50 min?
   c) Make your bed.
   • 2 min or 45 min?

3. a) Name 2 activities that could be done in 1 min.
   b) Name 2 activities that could be done in 1 h.

4. a) Name 2 activities you would not measure in minutes.
   b) Name 2 activities you would not measure in hours.

5. Suppose you do not have a clock or other timer.
   Use pictures, words, or numbers to show your thinking.
   a) How would you be able to tell when about 5 min has passed?
   b) How would you be able to tell when about 1 h has passed?

6. Ned visited his grandpa for 1 h.
   They spent 40 min ice fishing.
   They spent the rest of the time snowshoeing.
   How long did Ned and his grandpa spend snowshoeing?

7. It took Aki 46 s to draw a walrus.
   It took Oliver 1 min to draw a walrus.
   Who took more time to draw the walrus?
   How much more time?

Math Link

Your World

Raymond Saunders is a Canadian clockmaker.
He made the famous Gastown Steam Clock in
Vancouver, and he made steam clocks in Whistler
and Port Coquitlam.

You can see inside the clock through its glass sides.
The clock whistles every 15 min when steam comes
out of its vents.

Reflect

How could you explain to a Grade 1 student how long
10 min is?

Exploring the Calendar

Tell what you know from looking at this **calendar** page.

 Explore ··

You will need a blank calendar page and 4 index cards.

➤ Choose a month.

• Create a calendar for that month.

• Plan activities for that month.
  Record the activities on the calendar.

• Write 4 questions on index cards
  about your calendar activities.

Show *and* Share

Trade calendars and questions with another pair of classmates.
Answer their questions using their calendar.

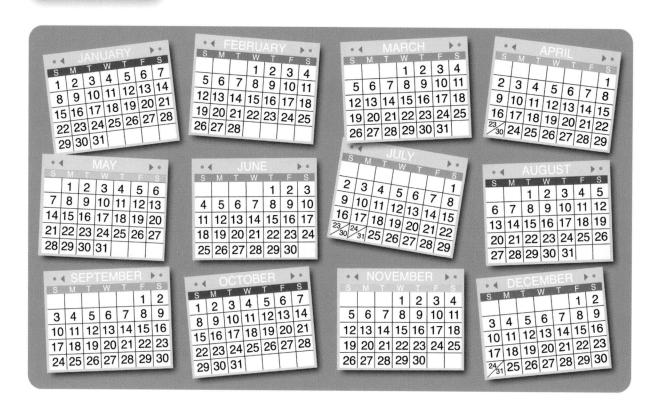

Each calendar page shows the days and
weeks of 1 month of the year.

Days, weeks, months, and years are units
of time.

The calendar pages show that:

➤ there are 7 months with 31 days
➤ there are 4 months with 30 days
➤ February has 28 days

> Once every 4 years,
> February has 29 days.
> These years are called
> leap years.

142

Practice

1. Name something you can do in:
   a) 1 day   **b)** 1 week   **c)** 1 month   **d)** 1 year

2. Which unit would you use to measure?
   Choose days, weeks, months, or years.
   a) how long it takes an apple seed to grow as tall as you
   b) how long it takes to learn to ride a bike
   c) how long you can borrow a book from the library
   d) how long a weekend is
   e) how long each season lasts
   f) the time from your seventh birthday to your eighth birthday

3. Which is longer? How do you know?
   a) 1 month or 2 weeks
   b) 1 week or 5 days
   c) October or June
   d) 16 days or 2 weeks

4. Aliy Zirkle was the first female to win the Yukon Quest sled dog race.
   She took 10 days, 22 hours, and 57 minutes.
   Did she take more than 2 weeks or less than 2 weeks? Explain.

Use a calendar to answer questions 5 to 8.

5. Suppose the Yukon Quest begins on February 9th.
   The winner crosses the finish line 12 days later.
   a) On what day of the week does the race begin?
   b) On what date does the winner cross the finish line?

Social Studies

There are many forms of this old poem.
It can help you remember the number of days in each month.
Do you know any other ways to remember?

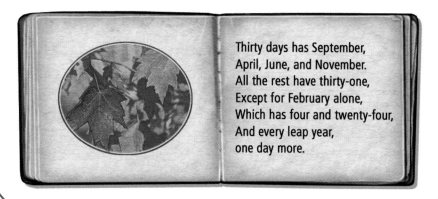

Thirty days has September,
April, June, and November.
All the rest have thirty-one,
Except for February alone,
Which has four and twenty-four,
And every leap year,
one day more.

6. **a)** Name the months with 31 days.
   b) Name the months with 30 days.
   c) How many Mondays are in July for this year?
   d) If you love Saturdays, which are your favourite months? Explain.

7. Hassan promised to do the dishes every day in March.
   Today is March 22, and he just finished the dishes.
   How many more days will Hassan do the dishes?

8. Canada celebrates National Aboriginal Day on June 21st.
   How long is it until the next National Aboriginal Day?

9. Tim and his family will go camping all July and August.
   How many days will they be gone? Show your thinking in pictures, numbers, or words.

Reflect

How would you find how much time has passed since your last birthday?
Explain what units you would use and why.

Using a Ruler

Why did Leo and Angie get different measurements?
What can they do so they both get the same measurement?

The table is 23 tiles long.

The table is 10 strips long.

Explore

You will need a long strip of tagboard, green and yellow
strips of paper, and glue.

➤ Make a tagboard ruler. Glue the colour strips along the top edge
of the tagboard. Use the pattern green, yellow, green, yellow, ...
Make the strips touch one another without overlapping.

➤ Use your tagboard ruler to measure the length of
   • a pencil
   • a desktop
   • your hand
   • your shoe
   • an object of your choice

What We Measured	Length
a pencil	almost 3 units
a desktop	

Show *and* Share

Share your results with another pair of classmates.

Why is it important for everyone to use the same units to measure lengths?
Which way do you prefer to measure? Explain.
- using objects
- using a tagboard ruler

A ruler is a tool for measuring length.

➤ The tagboard ruler uses paper strip units.

The pencil case is about 4 units long.

➤ This ruler is marked in **centimetres** (cm).

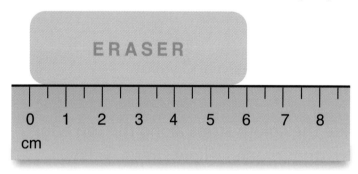

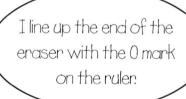

I line up the end of the eraser with the 0 mark on the ruler.

The eraser is 6 cm long.

Centimetres are standard units used to measure length.
They help us to understand everybody's results.

You can use a ruler to draw a line of a given length.

Start at 0 cm.
Trace along the ruler to the length you want.

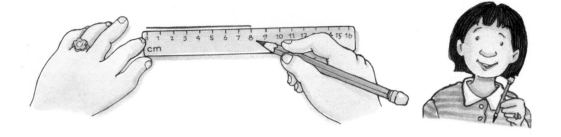

The line I drew is 8 cm long.

Practice

Use a centimetre ruler for questions 1 to 4.

1. Find 2 objects that are each between 10 cm and 20 cm long. Measure each object. Record your results.

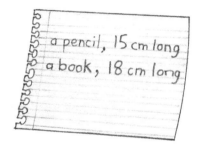

a pencil, 15 cm long
a book, 18 cm long

2. Find 3 classroom objects so that
   • 1 is less than 25 cm long
   • 1 is greater than 25 cm long
   • 1 is very close to 25 cm long
   Record your results.

3. Measure the length of each shape.
   a)

   b)

   c)

4. Draw a line for each fact to show how long or how high. Label each line.

   a) A grasshopper is about 6 cm long.

   b) It can jump up to a height of about 25 cm.

   c) In Canada, beetles grow to about 3 cm in length.

   d) They can jump almost 11 cm high.

   e) In South America, beetles can grow more than 13 cm long.

5. Without using a ruler, draw a line that is about

   a) 11 cm   **b)** 3 cm   **c)** 10 cm

Then measure each line to see how you did.

6. Arlo says that this line is 12 cm long. Do you agree with Arlo? Explain.

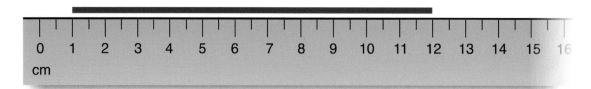

7. Marcella says that this crayon is 8 cm long. Is she right? How do you know?

Reflect

What are some good reasons for measuring length using centimetres instead of other units such as paper strips? Use pictures or words to give your reasons.

Estimating and Measuring with Centimetres

This crayon is **longer** than 6 cm but **shorter** than 7 cm.
The crayon is about 6 cm long.

Explore

You will need a 30-cm ruler or a measuring tape.

➤ Estimate, and record, the length of
  • your hand
  • your thumb
  • your arm
  • your foot

➤ Measure, and record, the length of each body part.
  How close were your estimates?

Here are 2 ways to record your work.
• Draw and label a picture.
• Make a list.

Tanya's arm is longer than the ruler.
I measure 30 cm, hold my spot, and
add on the next measurement.

Show *and* Share

Talk to your partner.

Suppose you lost your ruler.
How could you use your measurements to find the width
of your textbook?

Connect

Centimetres can be used to measure how long,
how tall, or how wide an object is.
Here are some referents to help you think
about centimetres.

A **referent** is an object you can think about to help you estimate a measurement.

Your finger is
about 1 cm wide.
Its **width** is 1 cm.

The counter is
about 100 cm tall.
Its **height** is 100 cm.

100 cm

10 cm

A Base Ten rod is
10 cm long.
Its **length** is 10 cm.

A referent helps you estimate even if you cannot reach the object.

Practice

1. Choose a referent you could use for 1 cm.
   Explain your choice.

2. Use your referent from question 1.
   Find each object below.
   Estimate its length or width.
   Explain how the referent helped you.
   a) a classmate's shoe   **b)** a bulletin board   **c)** a marker

   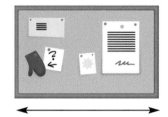   

3. Find each object.
   Measure its length and its width or height.
   Record each measurement.
   a) a paper clip   **b)** scissors   **c)** a tabletop

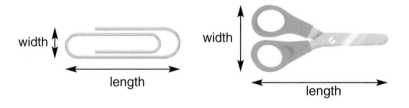   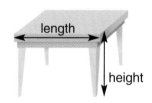

4. Choose an object.
   Measure its height, length, and width.
   Record your results.

Object	Height	Length	Width
bookshelf			

5. **a)** Name an object that is about 10 cm long.
   b) Name an object that is about 50 cm high.
   How do you know your estimates are close?

6. What is the length of each strip of paper? How do you know?

a)

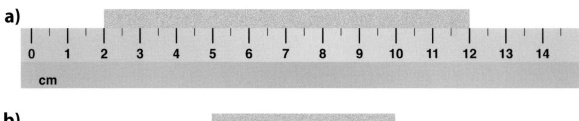

b)

c)

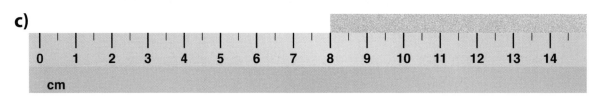

7. Daniel broke his ruler.

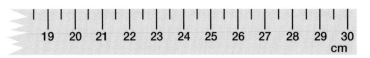

How can Daniel use his broken ruler
to measure the length and width of his desk?

8. A small paper clip is about 3 cm long.
A large paper clip is about 5 cm long.
How many of each paper clip would fit
along a 30-cm ruler?
How do you know?

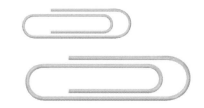

At Home

Reflect

Suppose you do not have a ruler.
How can you tell if a pencil is
longer or shorter than 10 cm?
Use words, pictures, or
numbers to explain.

You know that your finger
is about 1 cm wide. Use
your fingers to measure
some things at home.
Draw pictures to show
what you measured.

Button to Button

You will need 2 buttons and a ruler or measuring tape.

The object of the game is to make the closer estimate of the distance between 2 buttons.

➤ Take turns. One player places the buttons any distance apart on a table.

➤ Both players estimate the number of centimetres between the buttons.

➤ Work together to measure the distance between the buttons.

➤ The player who is closer without going over scores a point.

➤ Play until one player has scored 5 points.
Play again if you wish.

Estimating and Measuring with Metres

Danika and Cara wanted to measure some longer objects. They found a measuring stick in the classroom.

The measuring stick is one **metre** long. We call it a metre stick. They found the bookcase is about two metres long.

Explore

Use a metre stick or a metre strip, and Base Ten rods.
Find how centimetres and metres are related.

Each Base Ten rod is 10 cm long.

Show *and* Share

Talk to another pair of students. Tell what you found out about centimetres and metres.

How can you use the metre stick to measure the classroom door? To measure your desk?

One **metre** (m) is a length of 100 cm.

$$1 \text{ m } = \text{ } 100 \text{ cm}$$

Here are some referents for the metre.
A baseball bat is about 1 m long.

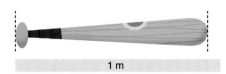

1 m

Lindsay is 3 years old.
She is about
1 m tall.

1 m

A **referent** can help you to estimate the
length of an object you cannot reach.

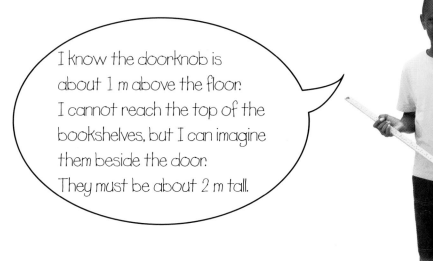

I know the doorknob is about 1 m above the floor. I cannot reach the top of the bookshelves, but I can imagine them beside the door. They must be about 2 m tall.

A refrigerator is about 150 cm tall.
You can write this as 1 m 50 cm.

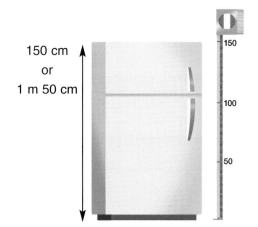

150 cm
or
1 m 50 cm

A minivan is about 180 cm wide
or 1 m 80 cm wide.

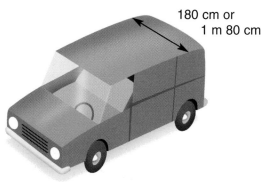

180 cm or
1 m 80 cm

1. Name 2 objects in your classroom that are taller than 1 m but shorter than 2 m.

2. Name an object that you can use as a referent for 1 m. Explain your choice.

3. Choose centimetres or metres to measure each item. Record your results.
   a) the height of your desk
   b) the length of a hallway
   c) the width of a hallway
   d) the length of your shoe

4. Use a measuring tape or metre stick. Find each object in your classroom. Measure and record.

   a) the length of the teacher's desk
   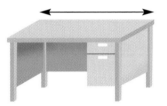

   b) the height of the classroom door

   c) the width of a window

5. Copy and complete this table. How could you use skip counting? What patterns do you see?

Metres	1	2	3	4	5	6	7	8	9	10
Centimetres	100									

6. Is the object a good referent for centimetres, or for metres?

    a) the height of a hockey net

    b) the width of a popsicle stick

    c) the width of a staple

    d) the width of a door

7. Suppose you found a stick that was 178 cm long.
Is its length closer to 1 m or 2 m?
How do you know?

8. The boys drew a chalk line on the sidewalk
that was longer than 1 m but shorter than 2 m.
How long might the line be?
How do you know?

9. Suppose you do not have a metre
stick, measuring tape, or metre strip.
How can you tell if an object is about 1 m long?

10. A pencil is 18 cm long.
About how many pencils like this would fit
end to end along a metre stick?
Explain your thinking.

At Home

Reflect

When would you *not* use
metres to measure?
Use words, pictures, or
numbers to explain.

Cut a piece of string 1 m
long. Bring your metre
string home and find
3 objects to measure
with it.

Strategies Toolkit

Explore

An ant crawled 6 m from its anthill to some crumbs. It picked up a crumb, crawled back to the anthill, and went back to the crumbs to pick up 1 more. Then the ant crawled back home. How far did the ant travel altogether?

Work together to solve this problem.

Show *and* Share

Describe the strategy you used to solve the problem.

Connect

Abby, Baba, Carl, and Dee live along the same hallway.
Abby's and Dee's doors are 20 m apart.
Baba's and Carl's doors are between Abby's and Dee's.
It is 8 m from Abby's door to Baba's door.
It is 4 m from Carl's door to Dee's door.
How far is it from Baba's door to Carl's door?

Strategies

- Make a chart.
- Use a model.
- Draw a picture.
- Solve a simpler problem.
- Work backward.
- Guess and test.
- Make an organized list.
- Use a pattern.

Understand

What do you know? It is:
- 20 m from Abby's door to Dee's.
- 8 m from Abby's door to Baba's.
- 4 m from Carl's door to Dee's.

Plan

Think of a strategy.
- You can **draw a picture** of the hall.
- Show each person's door in the hall.

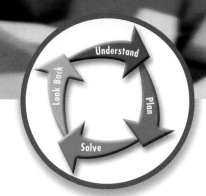

On the picture, record the distances you know. Find how far it is from Baba's door to Carl's door.

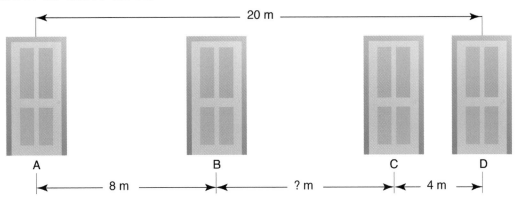

20 m

A   B   C   D

8 m   ? m   4 m

Do the distances from A to B and B to C and C to D add up to 20 m?

How could you have solved this problem a different way?

Practice

Choose one of the

Strategies

1. Winnie is 6 cm taller than Xenia.
   Xenia is 10 cm taller than Zack.
   Winnie is 132 cm tall.
   How tall is Zack?

2. Mia's garden has 3 sides. Its sides are 5 m, 7 m, and 5 m long.
   Mia planted zinnias 1 m apart around the edge of the garden.
   How many zinnias did Mia plant?

Reflect

Explain how drawing a picture helps you solve a problem.

Measuring Perimeter in Centimetres

Ellen is gluing coloured wool around this picture frame.

What length of wool does Ellen need to go around the frame?

The distance around the frame is its **perimeter**.

5 cm

7 cm

7 cm

5 cm

Explore

You will need a ruler.

➤ Look at 12 cm on the ruler. Look for something that you think has a perimeter of 12 cm. Measure the object to check your estimate.

➤ Look for another object with a perimeter of 12 cm.

➤ Now, look for objects with a perimeter of
• 20 cm
• 50 cm

Record your work.

Show and Share

Share your work with another pair of classmates.
Show how you measured a perimeter.

Connect

➤ Kay's group found the perimeter of a hockey card.
Each one in the group found a different way to measure.

> I measured each side,
> and then I added.
> 9 + 5 + 9 + 5 = 28
> The perimeter is 28 cm.

> I started at
> 1 corner, and turned
> my ruler at each
> corner until I got to
> my starting point.
> I measured off
> 28 cm altogether.

> I wrapped my
> measuring tape
> along the edges
> of the card.
> I measured off
> 28 cm altogether.

➤ Jeff's group found the perimeter of a square tile.

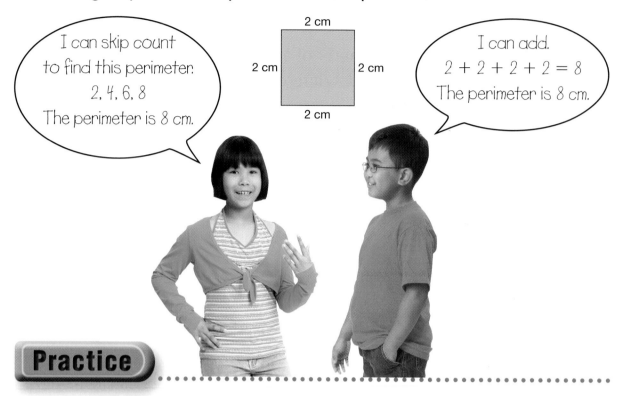

Practice

Use a ruler when you need to.

1. Estimate the perimeter of each shape.

   a)   b)   c)

   Measure to check each estimate.

2. Use 1-cm grid paper. Draw a shape with each perimeter.
   a) 8 cm   b) 12 cm   c) 10 cm   d) 14 cm

3. Measure and record the perimeter of each shape.
   Explain the strategy you used.

   a)   b)

   c)   d)

   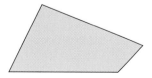
   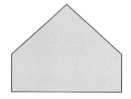

4. The perimeter of a square is 24 cm.
   How long is each side?
   How do you know?

5. Choose 3 different books.
   Estimate, then measure the perimeter of each book cover.
   Write the perimeters in order from least to greatest.

6. Find 2 objects so that the perimeter of one is about 10 cm
   shorter than the perimeter of the other.
   Record the name of each object.
   Record the perimeters.

7. Trace your shoe on paper.
   Find a way to measure the perimeter of your tracing.
   Explain your method.

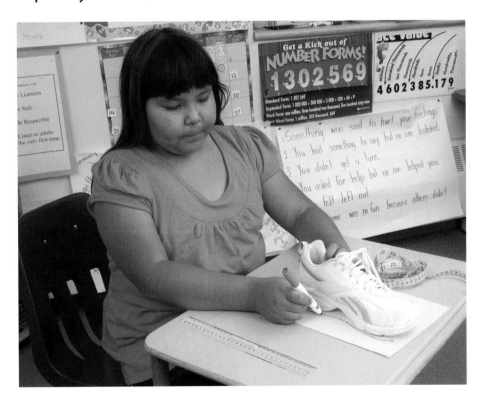

Reflect

Suppose an ant travelled along the perimeter of your pencil
case. Use words, pictures, or numbers to explain how you can
find the distance the ant travelled.

LESSON 9

Measuring Perimeter in Metres

Look around your classroom for something that you think has a perimeter greater than 1 m.
• Look at the doors and windows.
• Look at the floors and ceilings.
What did you find?

You will need metre sticks, metre strips, or measuring tapes.
Choose a region of the school.
You could look in
• your classroom
• the gym
• the library
• a hallway

Estimate the perimeter of the region in metres.
Plan how to find its perimeter.
Find its perimeter.
Record your results.

Show and Share

Share your work with another group.
Show the group how you found the perimeter.
Describe any estimation strategies you used.

Once I measured one side, I could estimate the next side.

➤ One group found the perimeter of this floor.

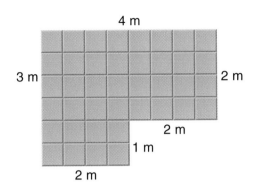

We measured each side, adding on as we went.

4 + 3 is 7.
Add on 2 is 9.
Add on 1 is 10.
10 + 2 is 12,
and 12 + 2 is 14.

The perimeter of the floor is 14 m.

➤ Another group found a shape on the Kindergarten floor.
They measured to find its perimeter.

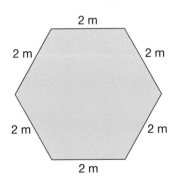

Each side is 2 m long.
I can skip count to
find the perimeter.
2, 4, 6, 8, 10, 12

The perimeter of the shape is 12 m.

1. Work with your group from *Explore*.
   Use metre sticks or metre strips.
   Form a shape with perimeter 6 m.
   Make a drawing of your shape, and label it.

2. Think of a referent for 1 m.
   Use your referent to estimate the perimeter of each item.
   a) your classroom floor
   b) a bulletin board
   c) a tabletop
   d) the classroom door

3. Choose an item from question 2.
   Find the perimeter, to the closest metre.
   Was your estimate high or low?

4. Liam bought 20 m of fencing to enclose his
   rectangular garden.
   How long and how wide could his garden be?
   Find at least 2 answers.
   Draw a picture to show your answers.

5. Would you use metres to find the perimeter
   of each item?
   Why or why not?
   a) a playing card
   b) your bedroom
   c) a playground
   d) your math book

Reflect

How do you decide whether to use centimetres or metres to
measure perimeter? Use words, pictures, or numbers to explain.

Exploring Shapes with Equal Perimeters

Explore

You will need square tiles and grid paper.
Make as many different shapes as you can with perimeter 12 units.
Colour squares on grid paper to show your shapes.

Show and Share

Show 2 classmates the shapes you made. What is the perimeter of each shape? How do you know each shape is different?

Connect

Different shapes can have the same perimeter.
Each of these shapes has perimeter 16 units.

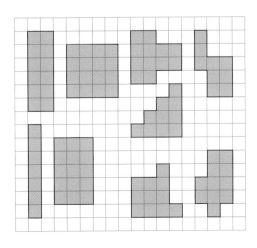

Use 1-cm grid paper for each question.

1. **a)** Draw different shapes with perimeter 18 cm.
   b) Draw different shapes with perimeter 8 cm.
   c) Draw different shapes with perimeter 14 cm.

2. Copy this shape on grid paper.
   Find its perimeter.
   Draw a different shape with the
   same perimeter.

3. Laila's garden has an unusual shape,
   but all of its corners are square.
   She has 24 m of fencing to put
   around the garden.
   Draw 3 different shapes on grid
   paper to show what Laila's
   garden might look like.

4. Draw a shape with perimeter 20 cm
   on 1-cm grid paper.
   Draw 2 more different shapes that also have
   perimeter 20 cm.

5. Work in a small group.
   You will need square tiles.
   Make as many shapes as you can with perimeter 10 units.
   Draw a picture of each shape.

Reflect

Use words, pictures, or numbers to show that many different
shapes can have the same perimeter.

Exploring Mass: The Kilogram

Some foods are sold by the **kilogram**.
This bag of rice measures one kilogram (1 kg).

Do you think you could lift this bag of rice?
Do you think you could lift 10 bags of rice like this?

Explore

You will need a balance scale, and
objects like the ones in the picture.

➤ Choose an object.
   Estimate. Do you think it is
   • lighter than 1 kg?
   • heavier than 1 kg?
   • about the same as 1 kg?

   Use the scale to check your
   estimate.

➤ Repeat with other objects.

➤ Record your work.

Show *and* Share

Talk about how you estimated.
Which objects were a little heavier
than 1 kg?
Which were a lot heavier?
How could you tell?

Lighter than 1 Kg	About 1 Kg	Heavier than 1 Kg
ball shoe	book	

When you measure how heavy an object is, you measure its **mass**. The kilogram (kg) is a unit of mass.

This chapter book has a mass of about 1 kg.

This case of iced tea has a mass of about 9 kg.

Practice

1. In your classroom, find an object that has a mass of about 1 kg. Use it as a referent to estimate the mass of each.
   a) your math book
   b) a dictionary
   c) your backpack
   d) your shoe

2. In your classroom, find
   • 3 objects that are less than 1 kg
   • 3 objects that are more than 1 kg
   Record your results.

Less than 1 Kg	More than 1 Kg

3. This giant frog lived at the time of the dinosaurs. It had a mass between 4 kg and 5 kg. Find something that has about the same mass. What can you tell about the size of the frog? Use words, pictures, or numbers to describe your ideas.

Reflect

Do bigger objects always have a greater mass than smaller objects? Explain your thinking.

Exploring Mass: The Gram

Hold a centimetre cube in your hand.
How would you describe its mass?
A centimetre cube has a mass of about one **gram**.
You write: 1 g

Explore

You will need objects like the ones in the picture.

➤ Choose an object.
Estimate its mass
in grams. Measure to
check your estimate.
Record your work.
Repeat with
other objects.

➤ Put a 1-kg mass
on the balance scale.
Estimate how many
grams it takes to balance 1 kg.
Check your estimate.
Write about what you found.

Show *and* Share

How did you decide which masses
to use to balance an object?

Object	Estimate of Mass	Mass
Nickel	9 g	4 g
Scissors	150 g	225 g

Connect

The gram is a small unit of mass.
The mass of an object you can hold in the palm of your hand
is usually measured in grams.

The bean seed has a mass of about 1 g.

A banana has a mass of about 200 g.

It takes 1000 g to balance 1 kg.

1000 g = 1 kg

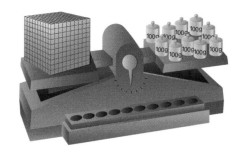

Practice

1. Name an object that has a mass of about 1 g.
   Explain your choice.
   Use your object as a referent to estimate the mass of each.
   a) a roll of 25 pennies
   b) a baseball
   c) an apple
   d) a mouse

2. Sort the objects into 2 groups
   • ones you would use as a referent for 1 g
   • ones you would use as a referent for 1 kg

   a counter   a book   a bottle of water   a dime

3. Would you use grams or kilograms to measure? Why?
   a) an eraser
   b) a chair
   c) a computer
   d) a pencil case

4. Name 2 objects that each have a mass of about 100 g.

5. Use a balance scale.
   Find the mass of an orange and a tennis ball.
   What did you discover?

6. a) Make a ball out of modelling clay.
   Use a balance scale to find its mass.
   b) Roll the ball of modelling clay between your hands
   to make a snake.
   Find the mass of the snake.
   c) What did you find out?

7. Bert's cookie recipe calls for 500 g of nuts.
   Will two 200-g bags be enough?
   Show your work.

8. Janet needs 1 kg of birdseed for her feeder.
   The store had only these sizes of bags:

Find 2 different ways Janet could buy the birdseed.
Show your work.

Reflect

Suppose you estimate the mass of an object.
How do you know if its mass will be measured in
grams or kilograms?
Use words, pictures, or numbers to explain.

LESSON

1
2

1. Which unit of time would you use to measure each activity?
  a) Playing a game of chess
    • pendulum swings or TV shows?
  b) Singing "Down by the Bay"
    • pendulum swings or recesses?
  c) Building an Inukshuk
    • seconds or minutes?
  d) Learning to ride a bike
    • days or months?

2
3

2. Choose the better estimate of time for each activity.
  a) Taking a shower, 5 min or 1 h?
  b) Building a snowman, 2 min or 15 min?
  c) Going on a camping trip, 5 days or 6 h?
  d) Growing tomatoes, 1 week or 3 months?
  e) Printing your name, 10 s or 1 min?

3

3. Yoshio's grandmother came to visit from Japan.
  She arrived on March 1st and left on June 30th.
  How many days did she visit?

4

4. Use a ruler. Draw a line 17 cm long.

5. How long is each object?

a)

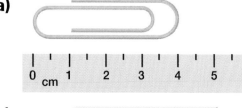

b)

c)

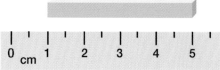

6. Use a ruler or a metre stick. Estimate.
Find an object that is
a) longer than 20 cm
b) shorter than 10 cm
c) longer than 1 m
Measure each object you found.
Record the name of each object and its length.

7. Find the perimeter of each object.
a) the cover of your math book
b) the longest tabletop in the classroom

8. Joe measured his garden and found its perimeter is 2000 cm.
What is another way of describing the perimeter
of Joe's garden?

9. Use 1-cm grid paper.
Draw as many shapes as you can with perimeter 16 cm.

10. Which unit would you use to measure
each mass?
a) a bag of oranges
b) a marble
c) a desk
d) a colour marker

11. Estimate the mass of each object.

a)

b)

c)

d)

U N I T
4 Learning Goals

- ✓ use non-standard and standard units to measure the passage of time
- ✓ use a calendar
- ✓ measure length, width, and height in centimetres and in metres
- ✓ measure perimeter in centimetres and in metres
- ✓ measure the mass of an object in grams and in kilograms

Eat Your Veggies

Part 1

Carrots are Yoko and Sandar's favourite vegetable.
What unit of time would they use to measure the time it takes
for each activity?

- planting a carrot seed
- building a scarecrow for the garden
- growing a carrot
- digging up a row of carrots
- peeling a carrot
- eating a raw carrot
- baking a carrot cake

Part 2

➤ Choose a vegetable.
  Measure the vegetable in as many ways as you can.
  Record your work in a chart.

➤ Repeat with 2 more vegetables.

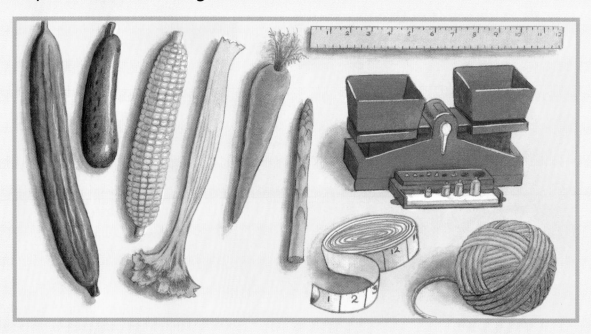

Part 3

➤ Suppose you want to plant a vegetable garden in the spring.
You need fencing around the garden to keep the rabbits out.
You have 18 m of fencing.
You want to use all of it.

➤ Use 1-cm grid paper.
Draw as many different gardens as you can that have perimeter 18 cm.

➤ Which garden shape would you choose? Why?

Check List

Your work should show
- ☑ how you used what you know about measuring
- ☑ your measurements recorded correctly, including units
- ☑ at least 3 different garden shapes drawn on grid paper
- ☑ a clear explanation of the garden shape you chose

Reflect on Your Learning

Write what you know about measuring time, length, perimeter, and mass.

How Many Buttons?

You will need the objects you see in this picture.

Don't have any buttons?
Choose another large collection like beads or counters.
Fill a box with your collection.

Part 1

➤ Look at the photo. What tools can you use to estimate the number of objects?

➤ Find as many ways to estimate as you can. Use words, numbers, or pictures to explain your plans.

Part 2

➤ Which way do you think will provide the best estimate? Why?

➤ Try it out. Get any materials you need.
Record your work.

Part 3

➤ Count the number of objects.
How can you group the objects to count them?

➤ How does your estimate compare with your count? Explain.

➤ How would you estimate differently next time? Explain.

Display Your Work

Report your findings using words, pictures, or numbers.

Take It Further

➤ Make a story problem based on your results.
Solve your problem.

➤ Trade problems with your partner.
Solve each other's problem.
Compare solutions.

Fractions

At the Pizza Shop

Today's Special - Arctic Char Pizza

Learning Goals

- find equal parts of a whole
- use fractions to describe parts of a whole
- represent fractions of a whole using concrete materials, pictures, and symbols
- compare fractions with the same denominators

Key Words

- equal parts
- fractions
- halves
- thirds
- quarters/fourths
- fifths
- sixths
- sevenths
- eighths
- ninths
- tenths
- numerator
- denominator

Look at the scene in the pizza shop.

- What things can you find that show a whole cut into equal parts? How many equal parts are there?

- How do you know the parts are equal?

Exploring Equal Parts

Think of sharing something
with a classmate.
How can you make sure
each of you gets a fair share?

Explore

You will need items like the ones in the picture.

- Make a plan for sharing each item equally with your partner.
- Share each item.
- Use pictures and words to describe how you shared.

Show *and* Share

Talk about how you decided to make fair shares.
How did you check to make sure the pieces were equal?
How would you make 3 fair shares? 4 fair shares?

When we share, we can make **equal parts**.

This orange is divided into 2 equal parts. It shows equal shares for 2 friends.

This pie is cut into 6 equal slices. It shows equal shares for 6 people.

Practice

1. Does each picture show equal parts? How do you know?

a)

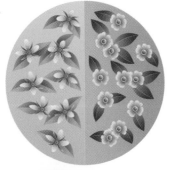

b)

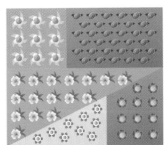

c)

Math Link

Social Studies

During the fur trade, French-Canadian voyageurs wore a sash, or *ceinture fléchée*, like this one. What patterns do you see in the sash?

2. Use a cutout of each shape.
Fold the shape to show equal parts.

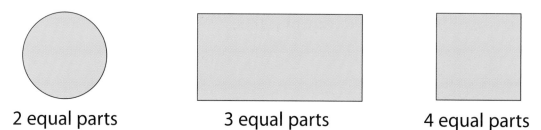

2 equal parts   3 equal parts   4 equal parts

3. Sort the pictures into 2 sets, those that show equal parts and those that do not. Use the letters to record your sorting. How can you check if a picture shows equal parts?

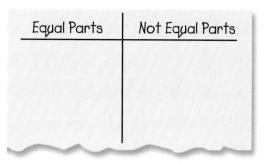

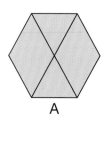 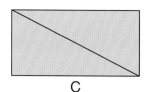 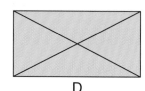

   A   B   C   D

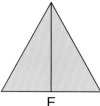 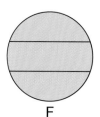  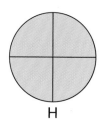

   E   F   G   H

4. Draw a picture of a whole object divided into equal parts. Use words to describe what your picture shows.

Reflect

Describe a time when you or someone you know divided a whole into equal parts.
How did you make sure the parts were equal?

Equal Parts of a Whole

Explore

You will need Pattern Blocks.

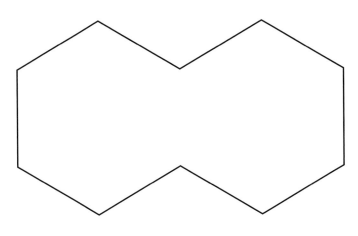

➤ How many ways can you cover this shape
with Pattern Blocks to show equal parts?
Tell about the equal parts each time.
Record your work.

➤ Repeat the activity with a shape you make
from Pattern Blocks.

Colour of blocks	Number of blocks
blue	6

Show *and* Share

Share your work with another pair of classmates.
Tell how you knew the parts were equal.

LESSON FOCUS | Describe equal parts of a whole as fractions.

185

➤ This shape is **1 whole**.

Here are some ways to divide the shape into equal parts.
You can name equal parts with **fractions**.

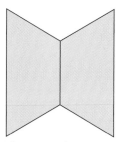

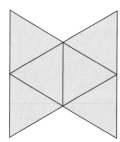

Fractions name equal
parts of a whole.

2 equal parts
2 halves

6 equal parts
6 sixths

➤ You can show the same fractions in many ways.
Here are some ways to show **fourths** or
quarters of 1 whole.

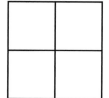
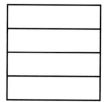
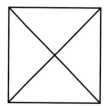

Practice •

1. Use Pattern Blocks to show equal parts
of this shape in 3 different ways.
Name the equal parts for each way.

2. Name the equal parts.
Tell why you think they are equal parts.

a) 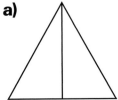   **b)**    **c)** 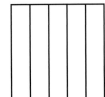   **d)**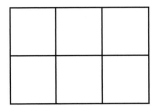

3. Which picture shows equal parts?
Name the equal parts.

a) 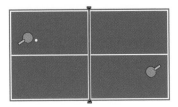   **b)**

4. Tell whether each picture shows fourths.
How do you know when it shows fourths?
How do you know when it does not?

a)   **b)** 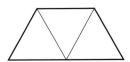   **c)**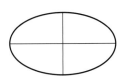

d)    **e)**   **f)**

5. a) Draw a shape on grid paper.
Fold your shape to show halves.
b) Draw a shape to show fifths.
c) Draw a shape to show fourths.
How can you tell you have equal parts
in each shape?

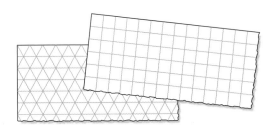

6. Imagine sharing a treat. Do you get a bigger piece when you share with many friends or with only a few? Show why your answer makes sense.

7. Describe 2 times when you have used fractions at home. Explain how you used them.

8. Draw a picture to show equal parts.
Name the parts.
How can you show the parts are equal?

9. How are these pictures the same?
How are they different?

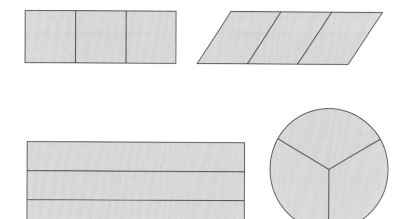

Reflect

What is your favourite strategy when checking for equal parts? How do you know your strategy works?

At Home

You have a pie to share at home. Show how to cut it so everybody gets an equal share.

Fractions of a Whole

Sami is using different colours of rods to show fractions.

You can do the same thing using rods or strips of coloured paper.

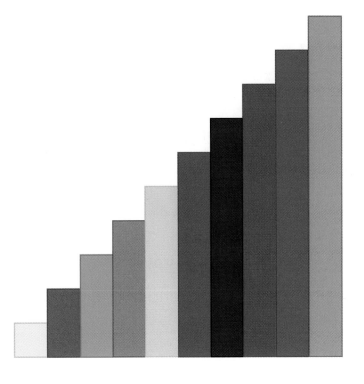

Explore

You will need rods or paper strips.

➤ Start with the orange rod.
Use the other rods to find different fractions of the orange rod.
How many ways can you do this?
Draw pictures and label them to record your work.

➤ Repeat the activity. Start with the blue rod.

You can use different rods for the whole.

Show and Share

Show your pictures to another pair of classmates.
How did you find equal parts?
How can you be sure you found all the possible fractions?

Connect

➤ Here is how Carey showed fractions of the dark green rod.

➤ You can fold a strip of paper to show fractions.

Carey knows the white rods are sixths because all of them are equal in length and there are 6 of them.

- Fold from end to end to show halves.

2 halves make 1 whole.

- Fold in half again to show fourths or quarters.

4 fourths make 1 whole.

- Fold in half again to show eighths.

8 eighths make 1 whole.

Once you fold the strip into equal parts, you can count the parts.

3 eighths   5 eighths

Use rods or paper strips when they help.

1. Which rod is 1 half of:

   a) the brown rod?   **b)** the purple rod?

2. Which rod is 1 third of:

   a) the light green rod?   **b)** the dark green rod?

3. Fold a sheet of paper into equal parts.
Name the parts.
Show a partner how you know the parts are equal.

4. What fraction of each strip is shaded?
What fraction is not shaded?

   a)

   b)

   c)

   d)

5. Draw and shade shapes to show:

   a) 1 half   **b)** 3 fourths   **c)** 2 thirds

Use pictures, words, and numbers to tell how you knew

   • how many parts to draw

   • how many parts to shade

6. Both Jay and Amira had a strip of paper.
Each child folded the strip into equal parts.
Jay had twice as many equal parts as Amira.
Use paper strips to model some possible fractions they used.

7. Could 1 third ever be larger than 1 half?
Make some examples using paper strips or rods.
Use pictures and words to show your ideas.

8. About what fraction of the race has each
person run? Explain.

Reflect

Use pictures, words, or numbers to explain the
fraction 2 fifths.

LESSON

Naming and Writing Fractions

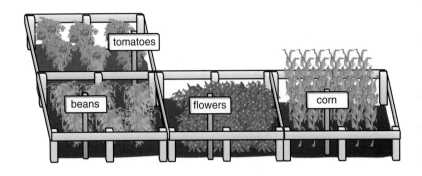

This community garden has 4 equal parts.
3 fourths of the garden are for growing food.

The fraction name suggests a symbol for writing the fraction.

$$\frac{3}{4} \quad \begin{array}{l} \leftarrow 3 \\ \leftarrow \text{of} \\ \leftarrow \text{4 equal parts are for growing food.} \end{array}$$

You will need grid paper, 10 blank cards, and scissors.
Make a fraction puzzle for your partner.

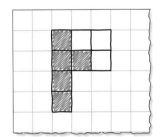

➤ Draw 5 different shapes on grid paper.
   Make each shape with a different number of squares.
   Cut the grid paper to separate the shapes.

➤ Colour a fraction of the squares on each shape.

➤ On one card, record the fraction
   using words.

➤ On another card, record the fraction
   using a symbol.

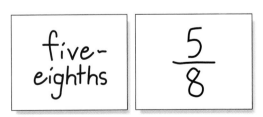

Show and Share

Mix up your shapes and cards. Trade with your partner.
Sort your partner's shapes and cards into 5 matching sets.
Check each other's work.

Connect

This shape has 7 squares,
so it shows sevenths.

Four of the 7 squares are coloured,
so the fraction is $\frac{4}{7}$.

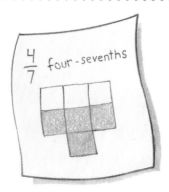

$$\frac{4}{7}$$

← The **top number** of a fraction tells how
many equal parts are counted.

← The **bottom number** of a fraction tells
how many equal parts are in the whole.

4 is the **numerator**.
7 is the **denominator**.

Practice

1. Use words and symbols. Write a fraction for the shaded part
   of each shape.

   a)

   b)
   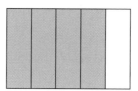

   c)
   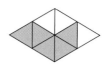

   d)

   e)
   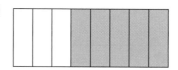

   f)

2. Choose 1 part from question 1.
   Name the denominator. Explain what it means.
   Name the numerator. Explain what it means.

3. How are the fractions in each set the same?
How are they different?

a) $\frac{3}{8}, \frac{1}{8}, \frac{6}{8}, \frac{4}{8}$

b) $\frac{5}{6}, \frac{2}{5}, \frac{5}{5}, \frac{3}{5}$

c) $\frac{4}{8}, \frac{4}{6}, \frac{4}{5}, \frac{4}{10}$

4. Sort these fractions into 2 sets: $\frac{5}{12}, \frac{2}{5}, \frac{3}{12}, \frac{1}{2}, \frac{7}{12}, \frac{4}{6}, \frac{1}{3}, \frac{11}{12}$

Explain your sorting rule.
Sort again, and explain your rule.

5. Kia's after-school centre is having a flag day to celebrate the children's different cultures.
Use fractions to describe each of these flags.

a)

Panama

b)

Nigeria

c)

Papua New Guinea

6. Draw a flag for each description.

a) $\frac{2}{3}$ yellow and $\frac{1}{3}$ blue

b) $\frac{2}{5}$ white, $\frac{1}{5}$ green, and $\frac{2}{5}$ black

Pick 1 of your answers. Describe how you used the fractions to draw your flag.

7. Ms. Chung has finished $\frac{1}{4}$ of her patio.
Use grid paper.
Draw a picture to show what the whole patio might look like.
Show 3 different ways you can do this.

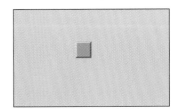

Reflect

Show a fraction on grid paper. Name the fraction.
Use your picture to explain the meaning
of *numerator* and *denominator*.

Three in a Row

You will need game boards, fraction cards, and counters.

The object of the game is to get 3 of your counters in a row in any direction.

➤ Players choose a game board.

➤ Shuffle the fraction cards and place them face down on the table.

➤ Player A draws a card and names the fraction.

➤ Any player who has that fraction on her game board covers the square with a counter.

➤ Players take turns to draw a card and name the fraction.

➤ The first player to get 3 counters in a row in any direction wins.

Comparing Fractions

What fraction of the yellow Pattern Block is the red
block? The blue block? The green block?
How do you know?

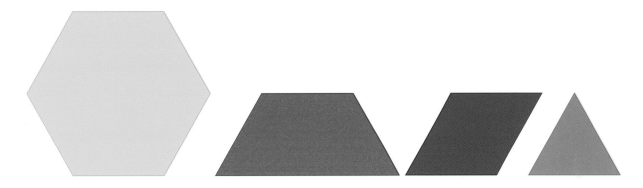

Explore

You will need Pattern Blocks.

Use the yellow Pattern Block as 1 whole.
Use other Pattern Blocks to make fractions.
Which fraction in each pair is greater?

$\frac{2}{3}$ and $\frac{1}{3}$ $\frac{1}{2}$ and $\frac{2}{2}$

$\frac{5}{6}$ and $\frac{3}{6}$ $\frac{1}{6}$ and $\frac{4}{6}$

$\frac{2}{3}$ and $\frac{3}{3}$ $\frac{6}{6}$ and $\frac{2}{6}$

Show *and* Share

Share your work with another pair of classmates.
How did you know which fraction in each pair was greater?

➤ When comparing fractions with the same denominator, look at the numerator.

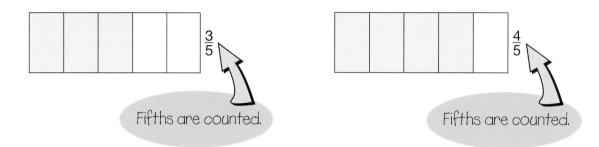

$\frac{3}{5}$ has fewer fifths than $\frac{4}{5}$.
So, $\frac{3}{5} < \frac{4}{5}$.

$\frac{4}{5}$ has more fifths than $\frac{3}{5}$.
So, $\frac{4}{5} > \frac{3}{5}$.

➤ Here is one way to compare $\frac{2}{6}$ and $\frac{5}{6}$.
Model each fraction with Pattern Blocks.

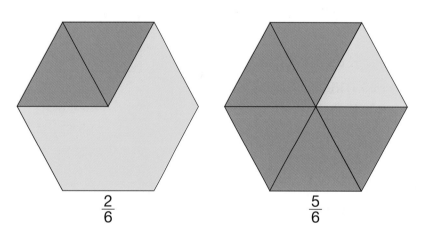

$$\frac{2}{6} \qquad\qquad \frac{5}{6}$$

Count the number of parts in each fraction.
2 parts are fewer than 5 parts.
So, $\frac{2}{6} < \frac{5}{6}$.

5 parts are more than 2 parts.
So, $\frac{5}{6} > \frac{2}{6}$.

1. Look at each pair of shapes.
   Write fractions to compare the shaded parts.
   Use >, <, or =.

   a)    **b)**   **c)**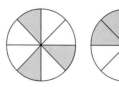

2. Use grid paper.
   Draw and shade shapes to show which is greater.

   a) $\frac{2}{3}$ or $\frac{1}{3}$ **b)** $\frac{4}{5}$ or $\frac{5}{5}$ **c)** $\frac{3}{4}$ or $\frac{2}{4}$

3. Draw pictures to show which is greater.

   a) $\frac{5}{8}$ or $\frac{3}{8}$ **b)** $\frac{2}{2}$ or $\frac{1}{2}$ **c)** $\frac{2}{6}$ or $\frac{5}{6}$

4. Use the red Pattern Block as 1 whole.
   Show which fraction is greater, $\frac{2}{3}$ or $\frac{3}{3}$.

5. Malka and Binda took part in a 3-day canoe trip.
   The first day Malka travelled $\frac{4}{10}$ of the total distance and
   Binda travelled $\frac{3}{10}$ of the total distance.
   Who travelled the greater distance?
   Draw a picture to show how you know.

6. On Tuesday, the Polar Bears hockey team
   practised for $\frac{7}{12}$ of an hour, and the
   Timber Wolves practised for $\frac{9}{12}$ of an hour.
   Which team spent more time practising?
   How do you know?

Reflect

Choose 2 different fractions with the same
denominator.
Draw pictures to show a friend how to compare them.

Strategies Toolkit

Explore

Amalie and Danny each have a sheet of coloured paper from the same pad. Amalie cuts her piece into fourths. Danny cuts his piece into sixths. Who has larger pieces?

Show *and* Share

Describe how you solved the problem.

Connect

Sébastien is making a picture with square tiles.
He has finished two-fifths of his picture.

Strategies

- **Make a chart.**
- **Use a model.**
- **Draw a picture.**
- **Solve a simpler problem.**
- **Work backward.**
- **Guess and test.**
- **Make an organized list.**
- **Use a pattern.**

What might be the shape of his finished picture?

What do you know?
- The square tiles are all the same size.
- Two-fifths of his picture is finished.

Think of a strategy to help you solve the problem.
- You can **use a model**.
- Choose materials to represent the square tiles.

Use your materials to model what Sébastien is doing.
- How many square tiles has he used so far?
- How many will he use altogether?

Show 3 different ways to solve the problem.

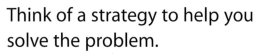

Choose one of the **Strategies**

1. Dusaka coloured a rectangle $\frac{1}{8}$ blue, $\frac{3}{8}$ green, and the rest orange.
   What fraction of the rectangle is orange?

2. Show how you can divide a square into 2 equal pieces.
   Find at least 2 ways.

Write about a time when you might want to find a fraction of a whole.
Use pictures, numbers, or words to explain.

1. Sort the pictures into 2 sets, those that show equal parts and those that do not. Use the letters to record your sorting.

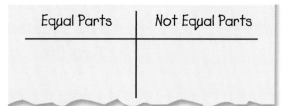

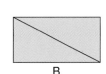

2. Which pictures show fourths? Which do not? How do you know?

a)
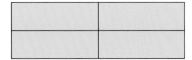

b)
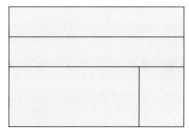

c)
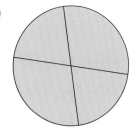

d)
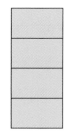

3. Fold a paper strip to show sixths.
   a) Colour 1 sixth of the strip.
   b) What fraction of the strip is **not** coloured?

4. Use symbols and words.
Write a fraction for each shaded part.
Write a fraction for each unshaded part.

a)

b)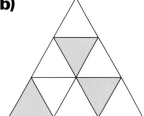

c)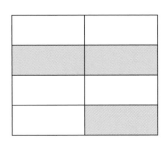

5. Draw a rectangle for each description.

a) $\frac{1}{3}$ blue and $\frac{2}{3}$ red

b) $\frac{1}{4}$ yellow, $\frac{1}{4}$ green, and $\frac{2}{4}$ blue

c) $\frac{1}{8}$ orange, $\frac{3}{8}$ black, and the rest green
What fraction is green?

6. Write fractions to compare the shaded
parts. Use >, <, or =.

a)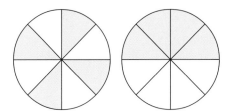

b)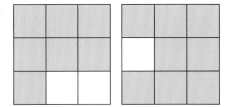

 UNIT

5 Learning Goals

✓ find equal parts of
a whole
✓ use fractions to describe
parts of a whole
✓ represent fractions of a
whole using concrete
materials, pictures, and
symbols
✓ compare fractions with the
same denominators

At the Pizza Shop

You have been hired to make pizzas at the local pizza shop.

One medium round pizza
4 slices mushroom only
4 slices pepperoni only

1 large rectangular pizza
6 slices pepperoni only
3 slices green peppers only
3 slices mushrooms only

1 small round pizza
2 slices ham only
2 slices sausage only

Part 1
Look at the pizza orders.
Use cutouts to model each pizza.
Make sure each pizza is cut into equal pieces.
Draw the toppings on the pizzas.
Use fractions to describe the parts of each pizza.

Part 2

Design your own pizza.
Cut it into as many equal pieces as you want.
Use any toppings you like.
Use fractions to describe your pizza.

Part 3

Sarah, Kon, and Nigel ordered a rectangle pizza with 12 slices.
Sarah ate 4 pieces and Kon and Nigel each ate 3 pieces.
Draw a picture to model the pizza.
Use fractions to tell how much of the pizza each person ate, and how much pizza was left over.

Reflect on Your Learning

Write about 1 important thing you learned about fractions.
Explain why it is important to know this.

Geometry

6

Under Construction

Learning Goals

- sort polygons by the number of sides
- describe objects by the shapes of the faces, and the number of faces, edges, and vertices

polygon

shape

object

face

edge

vertex, vertices

base

skeleton

prism

cube

pyramid

cone

sphere

cylinder

triangle

quadrilateral

pentagon

hexagon

octagon

The people of a medieval village are constructing the walls of their landowner's castle.

• Which shapes and objects do you see?
• How are some of the shapes different? The same?
• How are some of the objects different? The same?
• What else can you say about the shapes and objects in this picture?

Naming Polygons

These are polygons.

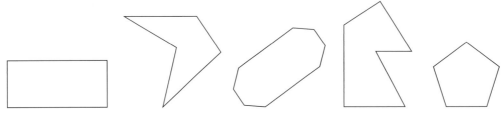

These are not polygons.

What is a polygon?
Look around your classroom. Find examples of polygons.

Explore

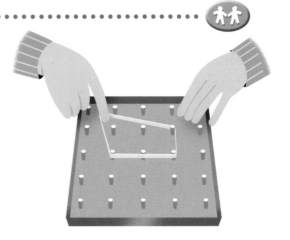

You will need geoboards, geobands, and geoboard paper.
Take turns.

➤ Make a polygon on the geoboard.
Ask your partner to describe it.
➤ Copy the polygon on geoboard paper.
Write about the polygon.
Repeat until you have made 6 polygons.

Show and Share

Compare your polygons with those of another pair of classmates.
Name any polygons you know.

Connect

Polygons have straight sides that are joined.

A polygon with 3 sides is a **triangle**.

A polygon with 4 sides is a **quadrilateral**.

Squares and rectangles are quadrilaterals.

A polygon with 5 sides is a **pentagon**.

A polygon with 6 sides is a **hexagon**.

A polygon with 8 sides is an **octagon**.

These are not polygons because the sides do not join, or not all the sides are straight.

1. Use a geoboard and geoboard paper.
   a) Make a quadrilateral inside an octagon.
   b) Make a pentagon and a hexagon that share a side.
   c) Make a triangle with sides that are different lengths.
   Copy your polygons on geoboard paper.

2. Use the polygons below.

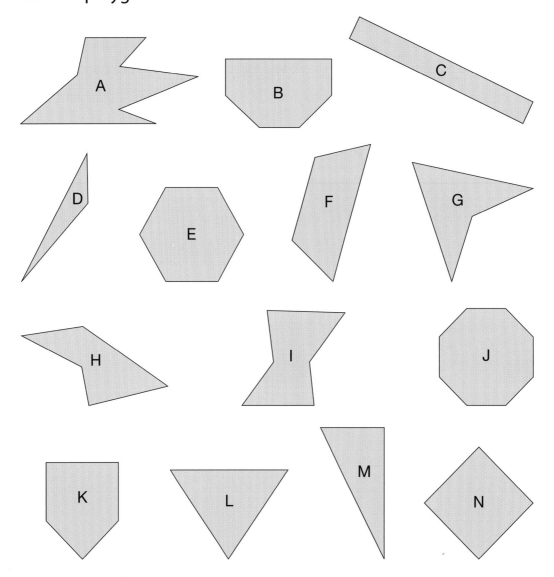

   a) Find 2 different quadrilaterals. How are they the same?
   b) Which polygons are hexagons?
      How do you know?
   c) Stephen says polygon A is an octagon.
      Do you agree? Explain.

3. Use the polygons from question 2.
   a) Copy and complete the chart.
   b) Choose 2 polygons that have the same number of sides. How are they the same? How are they different?
   c) When you name a polygon, does the length of the sides matter? Use examples to explain.

Number of Sides	Polygons	Name of Polygons
3		
4		
5		
6		
8		

4. What is the name of each polygon?
   a) A polygon with 8 sides
   b) A polygon with 6 sides
   c) A polygon with 3 sides that are the same length
   d) A polygon with 3 sides that are different lengths

5. Use dot paper. Draw these polygons.
   a) 2 different quadrilaterals
   b) 2 different hexagons
   c) 2 different triangles
   d) 2 different pentagons

6. Choose one part from question 5. Describe the 2 polygons you drew. Tell how you know they have the same name.

At Home

Reflect

Can a polygon have fewer than 3 sides? Use words, pictures, or numbers to explain.

Look around your home for polygons. Name any polygons you see.

Sorting Polygons

You will need large cutouts of these polygons.

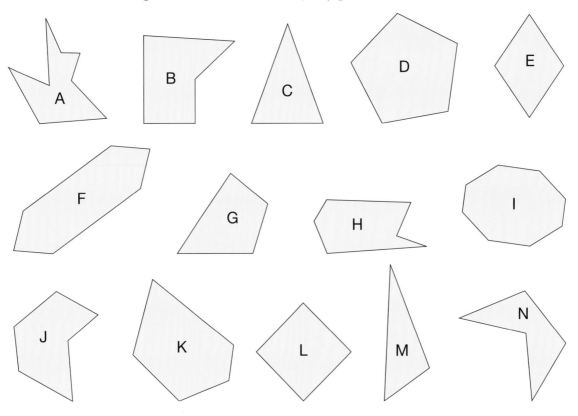

➤ Sort the polygons into 2 or more sets.
  Use the letters to record your sorting.
  Explain how you sorted.
➤ Repeat the activity.
  Sort the polygons a different way.

Show *and* Share

Share your sorting with another group of classmates.
Talk about how you sorted the polygons.

You can sort polygons by the number of sides.

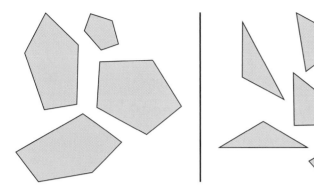

 The sorting rule is:

Polygons with 5 sides and polygons
with 3 sides

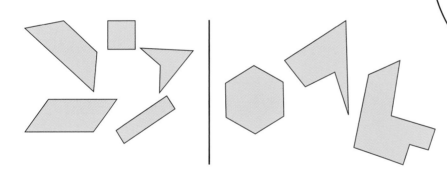

 The sorting rule is:

Polygons with 4 sides and polygons
with more than 4 sides

The polygons
with 4 sides are
quadrilaterals.
The other set of
polygons has a
pentagon, a hexagon,
and an octagon.

Practice •

For questions 1 and 2, use the polygons from *Explore*.

1. Sort the polygons for each sorting rule.
   Use the letters to record your sorting.
   a) Polygons with 3 sides and polygons with 6 sides
   b) Polygons with fewer than 5 sides and polygons with 8 sides
   c) Quadrilaterals and polygons that are not quadrilaterals

2. Secret Sort

 Game

Sort the polygons using a secret sorting rule.
Ask a classmate to say the sorting rule.
If the sorting rule is incorrect, you get 1 point.
If the sorting rule is correct, your classmate gets 1 point.
Repeat the activity. Take turns. See who can reach 5 points first.

3. Jerda sorted polygons into 2 sets by the number of sides.
Did she sort the polygons correctly? How do you know?

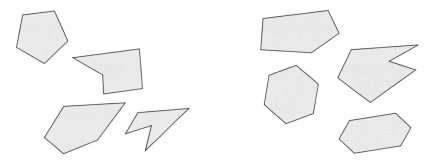

4. a) Carl put these polygons together.
What is the sorting rule?

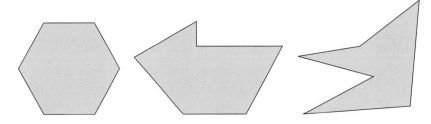

b) Which of the polygons below belong in Carl's set?
How do you know?

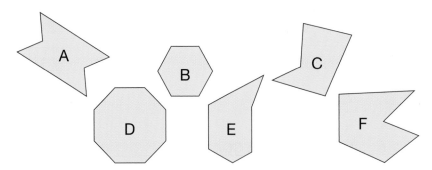

c) Which of the polygons in part b do not belong in Carl's set?
How do you know?

d) Sketch a polygon that belongs in Carl's set.
How do you know it belongs?

5. Choose 2 labelled cards.

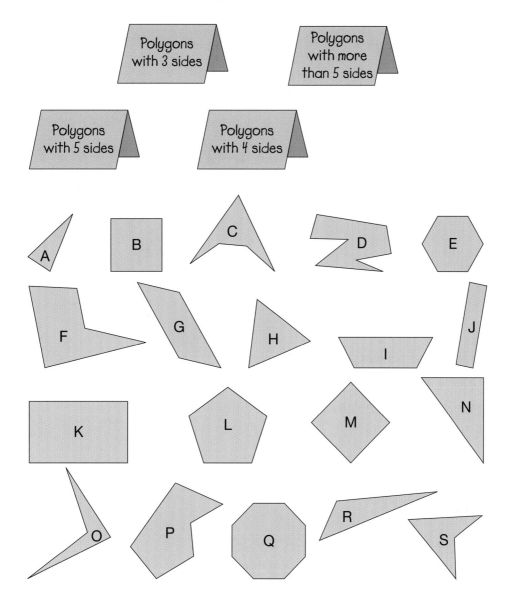

Use the sorting rules on the cards you chose.
Sort as many of the polygons as possible.
Use the letters to record your sorting.
Choose 2 different cards.
Sort the polygons again.

Reflect

What strategy do you use to keep track of which sides
of a polygon you have already counted?
Use pictures, numbers, or words to explain.

Strategies Toolkit

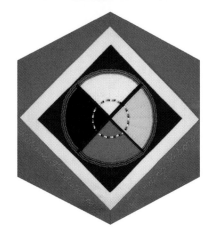

The Quilt of Belonging represents all of
Canada's First Peoples.
"Medicine Wheel" is a block from the quilt.
What polygons do you see?

Explore

Choose any 3 Pattern Blocks.
- Put the blocks next to each
  other to make a polygon.
- Use the same 3 blocks to make
  different polygons.
- Sketch your polygons.

You can do this.

You **cannot** do this.

Show *and* Share

Share your work with another pair of classmates.
Challenge your classmates to make a different
polygon with your blocks.

Connect

Use 1 green, 1 orange, and 1 red Pattern Block.
What different hexagons can you make?

Understand

What do you know?
- You must use 1 green, 1 orange, and
  1 red Pattern Block.
- You must make hexagons.

Strategies

- **Make a chart.**
- **Use a model.**
- **Draw a picture.**
- **Solve a simpler problem.**
- **Work backward.**
- **Guess and test.**
- **Make an organized list.**
- **Use a pattern.**

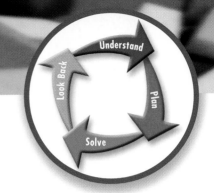

Think of a strategy to help you solve the problem.
- You can use **guess and test** to make hexagons.

- Arrange the Pattern Blocks to make a hexagon.
- Count the number of sides.
- If the polygon is a hexagon, sketch it. If the polygon is not a hexagon, try again.

Check your work.
Did you make hexagons? How do you know?

Practice

Choose one of the

Strategies

1. Think about the polygons you know. Which ones can you make using any 2 Pattern Blocks? Show your work.

We know triangle, quadrilateral,...

...pentagon, hexagon, and octagon.

2. Make quadrilaterals with:
   - 3 Pattern Blocks,
   - 4 Pattern Blocks, and
   - 5 Pattern Blocks.
   What different quadrilaterals can you make?

Reflect

Which polygons did you find the easiest to make? The most difficult? Explain.

Describing Prisms and Pyramids

This looks like a **pyramid**.

This looks like a **prism**.

How are the objects the same? How are they different?

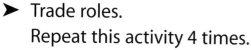
Explore

➤ Choose an object from the picture.
Keep your object secret.
Give your partner 3 clues about the object.
Ask your partner to guess the object.
➤ Trade roles.
Repeat this activity 4 times.

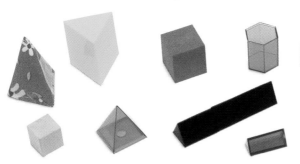

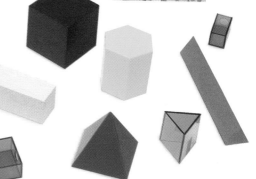

Show *and* Share

Share with your partner how you guessed each object.
Which clues did you find the most helpful?

➤ A pyramid has 1 **base**. The base is a **face**.
  A pyramid has some faces that are triangles.

This pyramid has 5 vertices,
8 edges, and 5 faces:
- 1 square
- 4 triangles

This pyramid has 7 vertices,
12 edges, and 7 faces:
- 1 hexagon
- 6 triangles

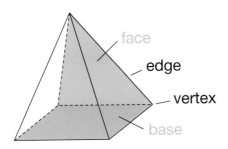

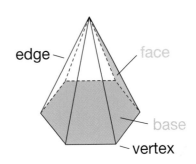

➤ A prism has 2 bases that are the same.
  A prism has some faces that are rectangles.

This prism has 6 vertices,
9 edges, and 5 faces:
- 2 triangles
- 3 rectangles

This prism has 10 vertices,
15 edges, and 7 faces:
- 2 pentagons
- 5 rectangles

A prism has rectangular faces.

A cube is a prism.
It has 8 vertices, 12 edges, and 6 square faces.

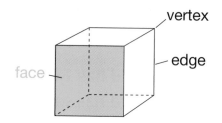

vertex

edge

face

Practice

1. Find objects like the ones in these pictures.
   Name the shapes of the faces on each pyramid.
   How many faces, edges, and vertices does each pyramid have?

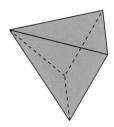 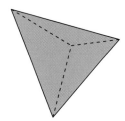 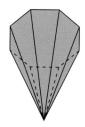

2. Find objects like the ones in these pictures.
   Name the shapes of the faces on each prism.
   How many faces, edges, and vertices does each prism have?

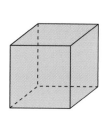 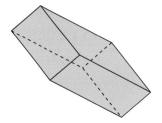 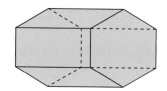

Math Link

Social Studies

In the Pacific Northwest, Aboriginal peoples used to make bentwood boxes to store things. Food, clothing, and ceremonial items were kept in boxes of all sizes. Today, the boxes are valued as works of art. The boxes are shaped like prisms.

Use models that look like these pictures for questions 3 and 4.

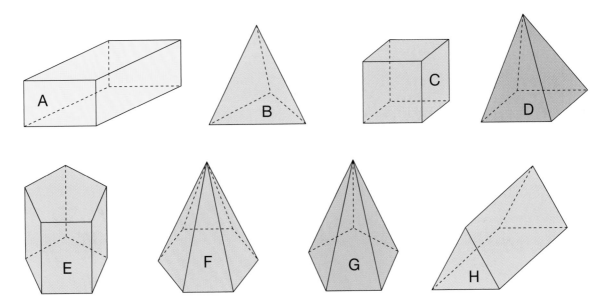

3. Which objects are prisms? Tell how you know.
   Choose a prism.
   How many faces, edges, and vertices does it have?

4. Which objects are pyramids? Tell how you know.
   Choose a pyramid.
   How many faces, edges, and vertices does it have?

 5. Ronda added labels to each picture.
   Did she label the pictures correctly?
   If not, what corrections would you make?

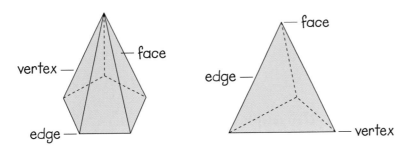

Reflect

How would you describe prisms to a classmate?
How would you describe pyramids to a classmate?

Describing Cylinders, Cones, and Spheres

This looks like a **cylinder**.

This looks like a **cone**.

This looks like a **sphere**.

How are the objects the same?
How are they different?

➤ Choose an object from the picture.
Keep your object secret.
Give your partner 3 clues
about the object.
Ask your partner to guess the object.

➤ Trade roles.
Repeat this activity 4 times.

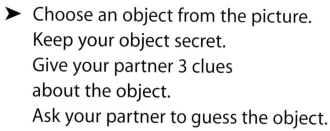

Show *and* Share

Share with your partner how you guessed each object.
Which clues did you find the most helpful?

A cone has 1 vertex, 1 edge, and
1 face that is a circle.

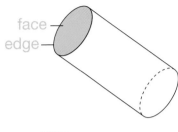

A cylinder has 0 vertices, 2 edges, and
2 faces that are circles.

A sphere has 0 vertices, 0 edges,
and 0 faces.

Practice

1. Copy and complete the chart.

	Name of Object	Number of Faces	Shape of Faces	Number of Edges	Number of Vertices

2. Yung added labels to each picture.
Did he label the pictures correctly? If not, what corrections would you make?

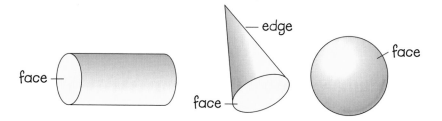

3. Is each sentence true or false?
Explain how you know.

    a) A cone has 0 edges and 1 face.

    b) A cylinder has 2 faces that are the same.

    c) A sphere has more vertices than edges.

4. Henri chose 3 objects from the picture below.
He counted a total of 4 faces, 4 edges, and 0 vertices.
Which objects did he choose? How do you know?
Use numbers and words to explain.

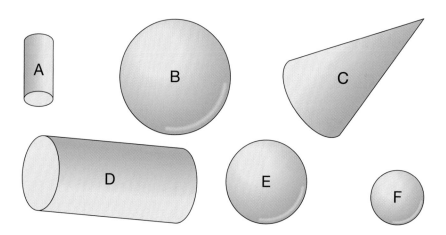

How would you describe cylinders, cones, and spheres to a classmate?
Use numbers and words to describe your thinking.

Sorting Objects

6

 **Explore** ···································

Use models of these objects.

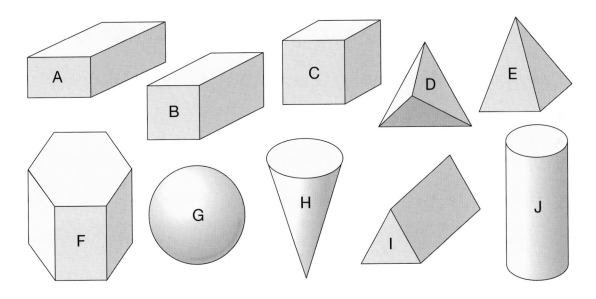

➤ Take turns sorting the objects.
➤ Ask your partner to tell the sorting rule you used.
   Record the sorting rule.
➤ Trade roles.

Show **and** Share

Show another pair of classmates one way you sorted.
Ask them to tell the sorting rule you used.

Connect

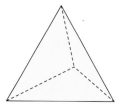

A cube has 6 faces, 8 vertices, and 12 edges.

This pyramid has 4 faces, 4 vertices, and 6 edges.

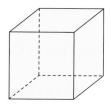

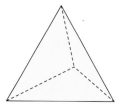

This pyramid has 5 faces, 5 vertices, and 8 edges.

This prism has 6 faces, 8 vertices, and 12 edges.

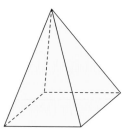

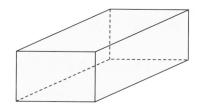

➤ One way to sort the objects above is shown below.

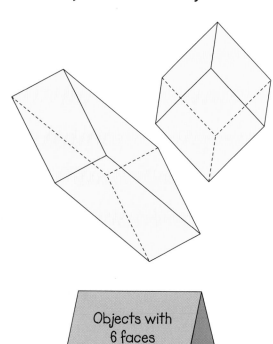

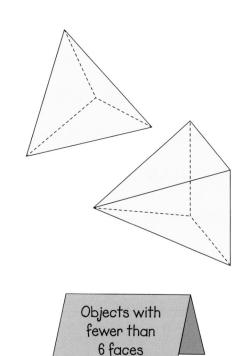

Objects with 6 faces

Objects with fewer than 6 faces

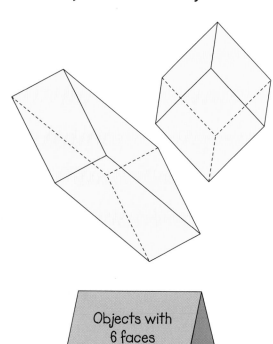
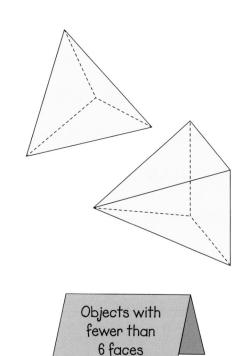

Use models when they help.

1. Sort the objects below using each sorting rule.
Use the letters to record your sorting.

   a) Objects with 6 faces and objects with 0 vertices

   b) Objects with 12 edges and objects with fewer than 6 vertices

   c) Objects with more than 6 edges and objects with fewer than 5 faces

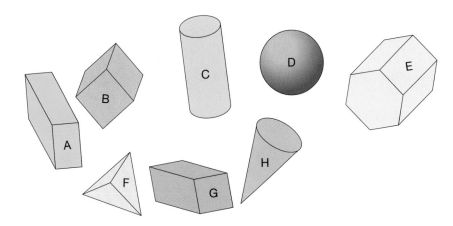

2. Norman sorted these objects. Write the sorting rule.
Compare your answer with that of a classmate.

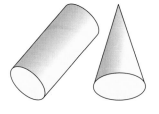

3. Use the objects from question 1.

   a) Sort the objects.
Write the sorting rule.

   b) Sort the objects again.
Write the new sorting rule.

Choose 5 different objects. Sort the objects.
Use numbers and words to explain how you sorted.

Guess My Object

You will need a bag, several small pieces of paper, and a variety of objects: pyramids, prisms, cones, cubes, cylinders, and spheres.

➤ Display the objects.

➤ Work together to write the names of the objects on pieces of paper. Fold the pieces of paper and put them in the bag.

➤ Player A secretly takes a paper from the bag. The object named on the paper is the mystery object.

➤ Player A gives 2 clues about the mystery object.

➤ The player who guesses the mystery object correctly gets a point.

➤ If none of the players guess correctly after 2 guesses, no one gets a point.

➤ Player A returns the piece of paper to the bag.

➤ The game continues until everyone has a chance to draw from the bag twice.

➤ The player with the most points wins.

Constructing Skeletons

When a building is constructed, the first step is to make a frame or **skeleton** of the building.

What can you tell about the skeleton?

You will need scissors, straws, modelling clay, and objects similar to the ones below.

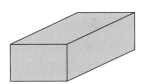
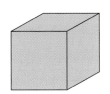
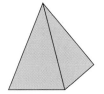
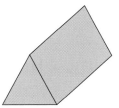

➤ Choose an object.
➤ Work together to make a skeleton that matches the object you chose.
➤ Choose a different object. Make a skeleton of it.
➤ Take turns describing each skeleton.

Show *and* Share

Show your skeletons to another pair of classmates.
Talk about how you made them.

A skeleton can be described by how many vertices and edges it has.

Skeleton	Number of Vertices	Number of Edges
Prism	8	12
Pyramid	5	8

All the faces on this prism are rectangles.

Practice •

Use models when it helps.

1. Jo made skeletons using toothpicks and balls of modelling clay.
    She counted edges and vertices.
    This chart shows some of Jo's results.
    Copy and complete her chart.

Number of Toothpicks	Number of Balls of Modelling clay	Skeleton
6		pyramid
	5	pyramid
9		prism
	8	prism
12		cube

2. Construct skeletons that match each description.
    Are you able to construct a skeleton each time? Explain.
    a) 6 vertices   b) 0 edges   c) 8 edges

3. Match the skeletons to the objects.
Explain how you know when a skeleton and an object match.
Construct a skeleton for any object that does not have a match.

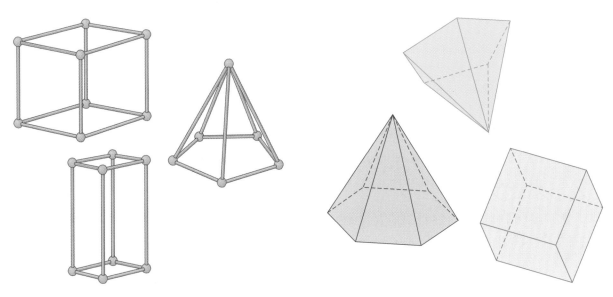

4. Get 20 toothpicks and 8 balls of clay.
You can use some or all of these materials, but
you cannot break the materials apart.
Construct a skeleton. Describe it.
Construct a different skeleton with a different
number of toothpicks and balls of clay.

5. Can you make a skeleton of a cone, a cylinder, or a sphere?
Explain why or why not.

Reflect

Choose an object.
Describe how you would construct a skeleton of it.

LESSON

1

1. Use dot paper. Draw these polygons.
   a) An octagon with some sides that are different lengths
   b) A pentagon with 3 sides that are the same length
   c) A triangle and a quadrilateral that share a side
   d) 2 different hexagons that share a side

2

2. a) Gerty sorted these polygons.
   What is the sorting rule?

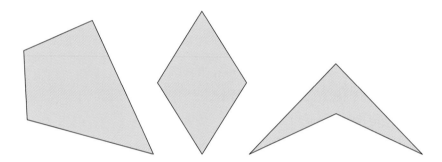

   b) Which of these polygons belong in Gerty's set?

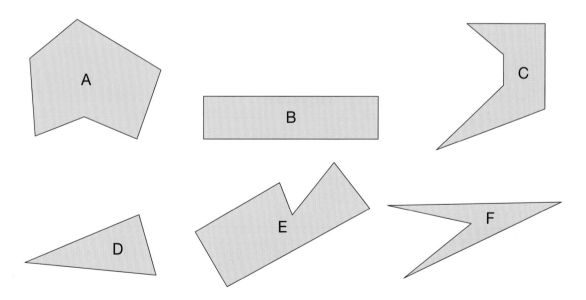

3. Use models of the objects in the picture.
Choose 2 objects. Name the shapes of the faces on each object.
How many faces, edges, and vertices does each object have?

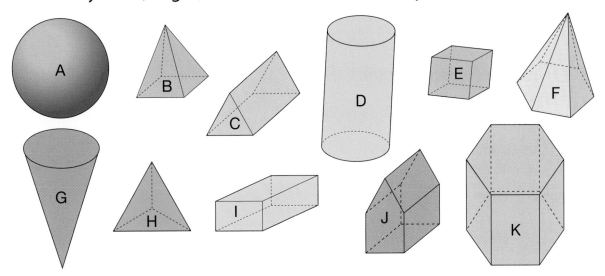

4. Is each sentence true or false?
Use numbers or words to explain your answers.
a) All pyramids have 3 faces.
b) Spheres have no vertices.
c) Some cones have 2 edges.
d) A prism has more edges and vertices than a cylinder.

6

5. a) Sort the objects in question 3.
Write the sorting rule.
b) Sort the objects again.
Write the new sorting rule.

7

6. Find objects like those in question 3.
Choose an object for which a skeleton
can be made.
Construct a skeleton of it.
Explain to a classmate how you made
the skeleton.

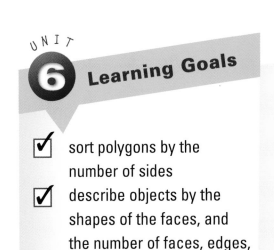

UNIT

6 Learning Goals

☑ sort polygons by the
number of sides
☑ describe objects by the
shapes of the faces, and
the number of faces, edges,
and vertices

Under Construction

Part 1

- Use objects, such as geometric models, cereal boxes, wooden blocks, straws, or cardboard tubes, to build a model of a castle.
- Explain how you made your castle.
- Choose 2 objects in your castle. Write what you know about each.

Part 2

- Use polygons and Pattern Blocks to add details, such as windows and doors.
- Choose any 2 of these polygons: triangle, quadrilateral, pentagon, hexagon, and octagon. Write about them.

Part 3

- Choose 1 object in your castle for which a skeleton can be made.
- Make the skeleton. Compare the skeleton and the object.

Your work should show
- ☑ the objects you learned about
- ☑ the polygons you learned about
- ☑ a description of objects and polygons
- ☑ a skeleton of an object

Reflect on Your Learning

Write what you know about polygons and objects. Use pictures, numbers, and words to explain your thinking.

UNIT

1 **1.** What are the next 3 numbers in each pattern?
 a) 67, 72, 77, 82, ...
 b) 99, 97, 95, 93, ...
 c) 12, 15, 18, 21, 24, 27, ...
 d) 64, 60, 56, 52, 48, 44, ...

2. a) How are these patterns the same? How are they different?
   25, 30, 35, 40, 45, 50, ...
   25, 35, 45, 55, ...
 b) Make another pattern that is different from both patterns in part a. Write your pattern rule.

2 **3.** Use Base Ten Blocks, or make a picture.
 Show each number 3 different ways.
 a) 327 b) 210 c) 583

4. Choose one number from question 3.
 a) Show the number on a place-value chart.
 b) Write the number in words.

5. Copy each pattern. Fill in the missing numbers.
 a) 325, ___, 375, 400, 425, ___, 475
 b) ___, 734, 730, 726, 722, ___, 714

3 **6.** Look at these numbers: 26, 85, 41, 73, 95, 24
 Estimate. Which 2 numbers have a sum closest to 100?
 Use pictures, words, or numbers to show your thinking.

7. Find two 3-digit numbers that have a difference of 234.
 Write a story problem for the numbers you chose.

8. Choose the better time estimate for each activity.
   a) A visit to the library: 4 min or 30 min?
   b) A school holiday: 2 weeks or 5 months?

9. Use a ruler, metre stick, or measuring tape. Find an object that is
   a) about 10 cm long
   b) about 1 m high
   c) about 30 cm wide
   Measure each object. Record your work.

10. Use square tiles and grid paper.
    Find 3 shapes that have a perimeter of 20 units.
    Draw the shapes on grid paper.

11. Make pictures to show a shape divided into fourths.
    Find 3 different ways.

12. Fold a paper strip to show fifths. Colour $\frac{3}{5}$ of the strip.
    What fraction of the strip is not coloured?

6

13. Name each object. Sort the objects. Write your sorting rule.

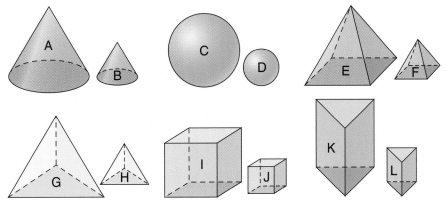

14. Solve each riddle.
    a) I am a polygon with 5 sides. What is my name?
    b) I am an object with 2 bases and 6 faces. What am I?
    c) I am an object with 1 face only. What am I?

Data Analysis

At the Vet

Learning Goals

- collect and organize data
- use tally marks, charts, lists, and line plots
- read bar graphs
- draw bar graphs
- use bar graphs to solve problems

FARM ANIMALS SEEN IN A DAY	
PLACE	NUMBER OF ANIMALS
Vet Clinic	|||||
Farms	||||| ||||| ||

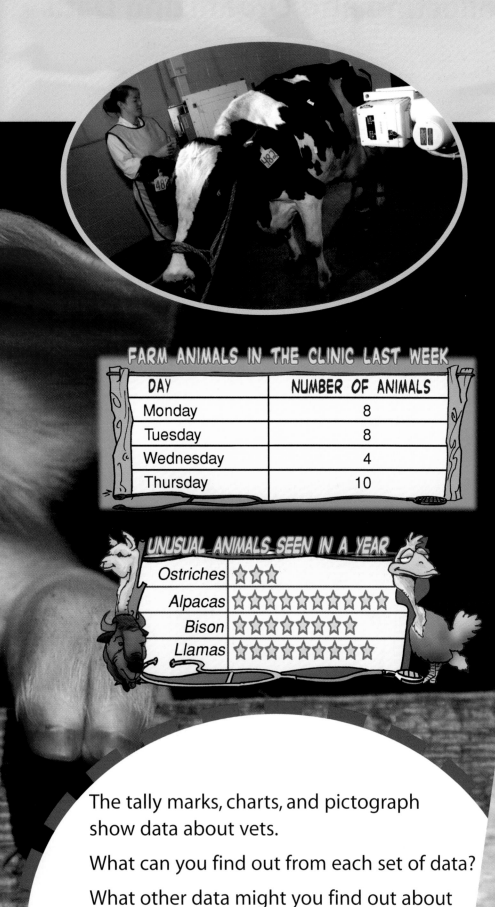

Key Words

data

chart

list

tally mark

tally chart

line plot

bar graph

title

axis (axes)

scale

FARM ANIMALS IN THE CLINIC LAST WEEK

DAY	NUMBER OF ANIMALS
Monday	8
Tuesday	8
Wednesday	4
Thursday	10

UNUSUAL ANIMALS SEEN IN A YEAR

Ostriches	☆☆☆
Alpacas	☆☆☆☆☆☆☆☆☆☆☆
Bison	☆☆☆☆☆☆☆☆
Llamas	☆☆☆☆☆☆☆☆☆

The tally marks, charts, and pictograph show data about vets.

What can you find out from each set of data?

What other data might you find out about farm animals or vets?

239

Collecting and Organizing Data

Data are facts or information.
Here are some ways to collect data.
• You can measure.
• You can count.
• You can ask questions.
You can collect data in a **chart**.

Explore

You will need a metre stick.

In your group, whose knee is
farthest from the ground?
Measure to find out.
Record your data in a chart.

Student	Ground to Knee

Measure each length
to the nearest
centimetre.

Show *and* Share

Share your results with
another group.
Whose knee is farthest
from the ground?
Closest to the ground?

You collect data to learn about people and things.
To collect data, begin with these questions:
- WHAT do you want to know?
- WHAT question will you ask?
- WHOM will you ask?
- HOW will you show what you find out?

You can record data in **tally charts** or **lists**.

Our Birthdays	
January	II
February	III
March	⊦⊦⊦⊦ II

Birds Spotted on Spring Days	
Day 1	4
Day 2	9
Day 3	3

Practice

1. Work with a partner.
   Measure the distance from elbow to fingertip on 5 classmates.
   Record your data in a chart.
   Whose elbow-to-fingertip distance is the longest? The shortest?

2. Yoshi asked his classmates to name their favourite fruit.
   a) Which fruit was the most popular? The least popular?
   b) Why did Yoshi include "Other" in his list?
   c) What else do you know from the data?

Our Favourite Fruit		
Fruit	Tally	Number of Children
Apple	IIII	4
Orange	⊦⊦⊦⊦ ⊦⊦⊦⊦	10
Banana	⊦⊦⊦⊦ II	7
Pear	II	2
Strawberry	⊦⊦⊦⊦ IIII	9
Other	IIII	4

3. Work with the class.
Are you wearing shoes with laces or shoes without laces?

Our Shoes

Shoes with laces	Shoes without laces

  a) Record your answer on the board.
  b) How many children are wearing shoes with laces?
  c) How many children are wearing shoes without laces?
  d) Are more children wearing shoes with laces or without laces?

4. a) Which animal in the chart jumps farthest? How far does it jump?

Animal Long Jump

Animal	Distance
Snowshoe Hare	3 m
Red Kangaroo	5 m
Cougar	9 m
Northern Leopard Frog	1 m

  b) How much farther does the kangaroo jump than the frog?
  c) Write 2 other questions about the data in the chart. Answer the questions.

5. Allie asked her classmates to wink. She organized the data in a list.

Our Winks

Closed Right Eye	Closed Left Eye
Tyler	Edith
Jessie	Avril
Madison	

  a) How many children closed their right eye?
  b) Write a question about Allie's list. Answer your question.
  c) Trade questions with a classmate. Compare answers.

6. Some children made these name tags.

a) Organize the names in lists by their first letters.
b) Which letter has the most names?
c) Organize the names a different way.
   Tell how you organized the names.
d) Write a question about your lists.
   Answer your question.

7. Which season do you and your classmates like best?
  a) Record your favourite season on the board.
  b) Record all the data in a tally chart.
  c) What did you find out? Explain.

Our Favourite Seasons		
Seasons	Tally	Number
Spring		
Summer		
Fall		
Winter		

8. a) Ask some classmates to say their favourite colour.
   b) Tell how you collected and organized the data.
   c) Write 3 things your data shows.

Reflect

Choose a *Practice* question from this lesson. Why might someone want to collect data about this question?

Line Plots

**Explore** ....

Natalie asked her classmates:

What is your favourite recess activity?
skipping ___   ball games ___
tag ___   hopscotch ___

She marked an X to show each choice.

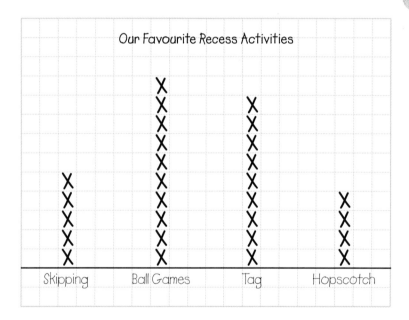

Our Favourite Recess Activities

| Skipping | Ball Games | Tag | Hopscotch |

Write 2 questions about Natalie's data.
Answer your questions.

Show and Share

Trade questions with another pair of classmates.
Answer the questions. Check each other's work.

A park is getting a new piece of playground equipment.
Monika's job is to choose the equipment.

She asks the children in the neighbourhood to help.
Each child can vote for 1 choice.

Monika uses these steps to make a **line plot** of the data.

➤ Draw a line on grid paper.
Write the types of playground
equipment below the line.

➤ Mark an X to show each vote.

➤ Write a title.

The line plot shows that more
children chose a slide than
any other type of playground
equipment.

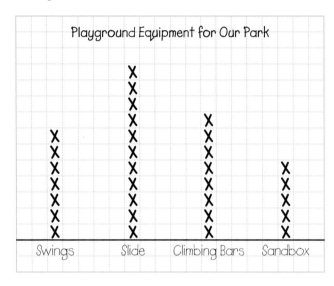

Playground Equipment for Our Park

The line plot shows that
11 children chose a slide.
You can use a line plot to make comparisons.

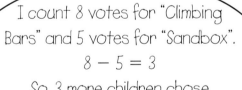

I count 8 votes for "Climbing
Bars" and 5 votes for "Sandbox".
8 − 5 = 3
So, 3 more children chose
climbing bars.

I see 3 more Xs
above "Climbing Bars."
So, 3 more children
chose climbing bars.

1. Blossom likes to go bird watching with her grandmother.
   She recorded the types of birds they saw in 1 week.

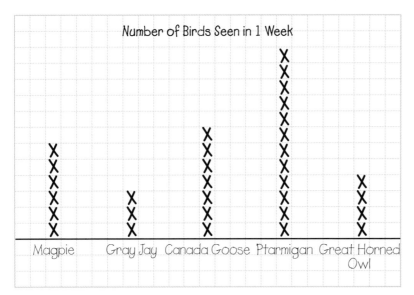

   a) Which type of bird did Blossom and her grandmother
      see most often? Least often?
      How do you know?
   b) Write 3 other things you know from the line plot.

2. Irina made this line plot to show the number
   of buttons on classmates' clothes.

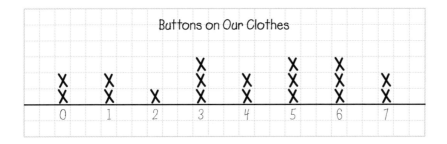

   a) How many children have 6 buttons?
   b) What is the most number of buttons for any child?
      How many children have this many buttons?
   c) Is everyone in the classroom wearing clothes with buttons?
      How does the line plot show this?

3. a) Ask some classmates:

Which playground equipment would you choose for a park?
swing set ___   slide ___   climbing bars ___

Collect and organize the data in a line plot.

b) Suppose you are choosing the equipment for the park.
What would you buy? Why?

4. Ethan listed shoe sizes of some Grade 3 children.
4, 5, 2, 3, 4, 5, 4, 2, 4, 3, 2, 1, 2, 1, 3, 4, 1, 2, 3, 4, 2, 3, 4
a) Show the data in a line plot.
b) Write what you know from the line plot.

5. a) Write the names of 8 of your classmates.
b) Show the number of letters in each name on a line plot.
c) Write 3 things you know from the line plot.

6. a) Choose a line plot from this lesson.
Draw the line plot with the labels in a
different order.
b) Are the data the same? Explain.

7. How are all the line plots in this lesson the same?

At Home

Reflect

How is a line plot the same as a
tally chart? How is it different?
Which do you like more? Why?

Think of something you would
like to know about your family
or friends.
Collect the data with a line
plot, chart, or list.
What did you find out?

Reading Bar Graphs

Henry takes photographs of Saskatchewan wildflowers.

Explore

Henry drew this graph about his photographs. List 5 things you know from looking at Henry's graph.

Show and Share

Share your list with another pair of classmates.

Why do you think Henry's graph is called a bar graph?

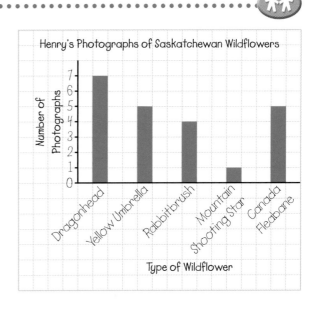

Henry's Photographs of Saskatchewan Wildflowers

Number of Photographs

Type of Wildflower

Andrea and Lim learned about some animals in British Columbia.
They drew bar graphs about their footprints.

Andrea's graph: Lim's graph:

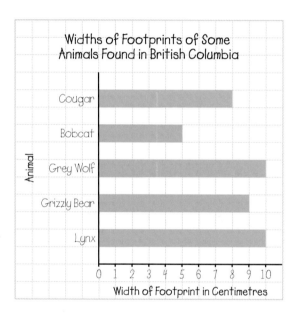

The **title** tells what the graph shows.

The labels on the **axes** tell about the data.

The numbers on the **axis** labelled "Width of Footprint in Centimetres" show the **scale**.
The scale is: 1 square represents a width of 1 cm.

On both bar graphs, the bars for
Cougar line up with 8.
So, the width of a cougar footprint is 8 cm.

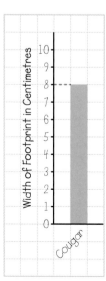

Practice

1. Eric's class voted on the type of tree to plant in their school yard.

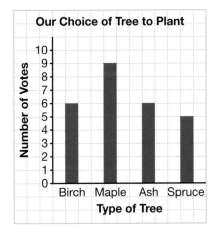

a) What do the labels on the axes tell you?

b) What does the graph tell you about the votes?

c) Which type of tree do you think the class will plant? Explain.

2. Lia asked classmates which season they like best.

a) Which season do most children like best?

b) How many classmates did Lia ask?

c) Write 2 other things you know from Lia's graph.

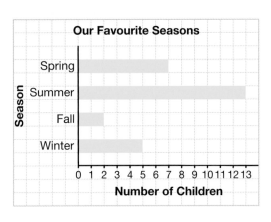

3. This bar graph shows the masses of some animals found in Canada.

a) Which animals have the same mass?

b) Order the masses from least to greatest. How did you do this?

c) What is the difference between the mass of a mink and the mass of a badger?

d) Write 2 questions about the data. Answer your questions.

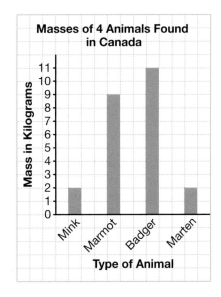

4. This graph shows the number of whales counted in some pods.

    a) What does each axis tell you?

    b) Write 3 things you know from this graph.

    c) Suppose there was 1 more whale in the Bowhead pod. How would the graph change?

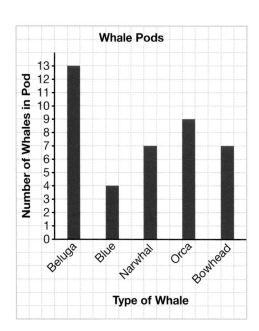

5. Frank made a bar graph about the goals scored by 3 teams in his soccer league.

    a) Which team scored the most goals? Describe how you can tell.

    b) Which line plot matches Frank's bar graph? How do you know?

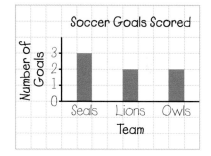

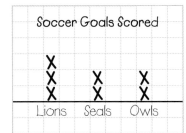
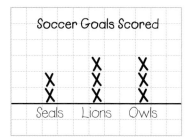
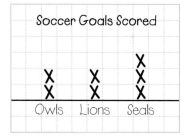

6. How are all the bar graphs in this lesson the same? How are some of the bar graphs different from others?

Reflect

Suppose the order of the bars in a graph is changed. Would the graph show the same data? Explain.

Drawing Bar Graphs

What types of movies do you and your classmates like best?

On the board, draw a **tally mark** beside the type of movie you like best.

Our Favourite Movies

Comedy ||
Action |||
Kids
Science Fiction |||
Drama
Mystery

Explore

You will need grid paper and a ruler.

➤ Use the tally marks on the board.
Draw a bar graph to show the movie data.
Colour 1 square to represent 1 choice.

➤ Write 3 questions about your graph.
Answer your questions.

Show *and* Share

Talk with another pair about how you drew the graphs.
How are the graphs the same? How are they different?
Discuss your questions and answers.

Elena asked her classmates:

What is your favourite activity to do at home?
play CDs ___
read ___
watch TV ___
play sports ___
use a computer ___
other ___

Favourite Activities to Do at Home

Activity	Tally	Number of Children
Play CDs	ⅢⅢ I	6
Read	IIII	4
Watch TV	III	3
Play sports	IIII	4
Use a computer	ⅢⅢ II	7
Other	II	2

To draw a bar graph:

➤ Draw 2 axes on grid paper.

➤ Write the title.

➤ Label one axis "Activity."
Write the names of the activities on this axis.

➤ Label the other axis "Number of Children."
Write the numbers along this axis.

➤ Colour 1 square over an activity for each child that chose it.

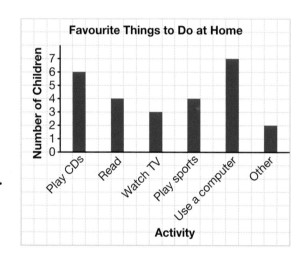

Here are some things we know from the graph:
• Using a computer was the most popular activity.
• The same number of children chose reading and playing sports.

1. Use the data in *Connect*.
   a) Draw a bar graph with the bars going sideways.
   b) Compare your bar graph with the one in *Connect*.

2. Emma asked her classmates who they would like to invite for lunch.
   a) Draw a bar graph to show the data.
   b) How many children altogether picked the top 2 choices?
   c) Suppose 2 of the children changed their answer from "Musician" to "RCMP officer." Tell how this would change your graph.

Lunch Guests	
Person	Number of Votes
Athlete	7
Nurse	4
Musician	6
RCMP officer	5

3. A class in Vancouver kept track of the number of days it snowed last year. They showed the data in a line plot.

Number of Days it Snowed in Vancouver Last Year

```
                    X
                    X
    X               X
    X               X
    X               X         X
    X               X         X              X
December        January     February      March
```

   a) Why do you think the class did not show the other months of the year in their line plot?
   b) Draw a bar graph to show the data.
   c) On how many days did Vancouver have snow?
   d) Write 2 other things you know from the bar graph.

4. Kumar wrote these data on the board.

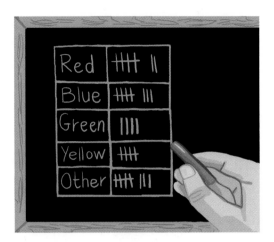

a) What do you think he asked the class?

b) Draw a bar graph for these data.

5. a) Draw a bar graph to show the data in the chart.

b) What is the difference in the lengths of the 2 shortest dinosaurs? Explain 2 ways to find the answer.

c) Write a question about the graph. Answer your question.

Lengths of Dinosaurs

Dinosaur	Body Length
Tyrannosaurus Rex	14 m
Albertosaurus	8 m
Triceratops	9 m
Ankylosaurus	10 m
Dromaeosaurus	2 m
Pachycephalosaurus	5 m

Reflect

What mistake do you think someone might make drawing a bar graph?

How would you correct the mistake?

Using Graphs to Solve Problems

➤ Talk about ways to find answers to these questions:
  • How many children in your class play sports?
  • Do your classmates prefer to watch sports or take part in sports?
  • What is the favourite sport of each child in your class?

 **Explore**

You will need grid paper and a ruler.

➤ Choose a question.
  • Which sport will your class watch on a trip to a high school?
  • Who will you invite to your class?
  • What sports will be in a sports day?

➤ In your group, talk about:
  • what question you will ask,
  • whom you will ask, and
  • how you will record the answers.

➤ Collect the data. Draw a bar graph.

➤ How will you answer your question?

> Which is your favourite sport to play?
> Hockey –
> Baseball –
> Basketball –
> Volleyball –
> Soccer –
> Other –

Show *and* Share

Share your question and data with another group.
Talk about your decisions.

Connect

Angie wanted to solve a problem about planning a class trip.

➤ Angie made a chart to collect data from her classmates.

I can organize the data in a tally chart or in a line plot. Let's see ... I think I'll use a tally chart.

Votes for Our Class Trip

Place	Tally	Number of Votes
Centre Park	III	3
Zoo	HHII IIII	9
Museum	HHI	5
Planetarium	IIII	4
Puppet Show	HHI	5

➤ She drew a graph.

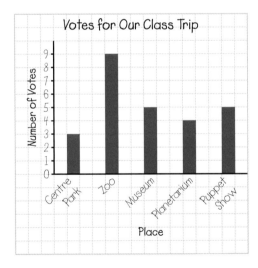

Angie found out:
- More children chose the zoo than any other place.
- The children's next choice was the museum or a puppet show.

So, Angie's solution was to plan a trip to the zoo.

1. Solve this problem.
   What trip would you plan for your classmates?
   a) List places to go.
      Decide if you want to use "Other" for children who prefer to go somewhere else.
   b) Collect and organize the data.
   c) Draw a bar graph to show your data.
   d) How would you solve the problem? Explain.

2. Choose a topic for a problem.
   a) Write the problem you will solve.
   b) What question will you ask?
   c) Collect and organize the data.
   d) Draw a bar graph to show your data.
   e) What is your solution for the problem? Tell how your graph helped you to solve the problem.

   > **Problem Topics**
   > - Story for the class to read together
   > - Game to play for indoor recess
   > - A visitor to invite to the classroom
   > - Music to play at a class party

3. a) Write a question about your problem and solution for question 2. Answer your question.
   b) Share your work with a classmate. Answer each other's questions. Compare answers.

Your World

Many kinds of graphs are used in newspapers, magazines, and on the Internet to show data.

Reflect

Describe a problem you solved in this lesson.
What would you do differently next time?

Reach Up or Sideways

You will need 2 number cubes, and a game board for each player.

The object of the game is to shade 6 squares in 1 bar, or to shade 1 square for each number from 0 to 12.

➤ Each player rolls a number cube.
   The player with the highest roll starts.

➤ On your turn, roll the number cubes. Add or subtract the numbers. Shade a square on your bar graph to show the answer.

➤ Take turns rolling the number cubes and shading a square.

➤ The winner is the first player to shade 6 squares in 1 bar, or to shade 1 square for each number from 0 to 12.

Strategies Toolkit

Explore ....

Shane had nickels, dimes, and quarters.
He bought a used comic book for 25¢.
He did not get any change.
How many different ways could
Shane have paid for the comic book?

Show *and* Share

Show your classmates how you solved the problem.
How do you know you have found all the different ways?

Connect ....

Amy had pennies, nickels, and dimes.
She bought a pencil for 20¢.
Amy did not get any change.
How many different ways could
Amy have paid for the pencil?

What do you know?
- Amy paid 20¢.
- Amy used pennies, nickels, and dimes.

Think of a strategy to help you solve the problem.
- You can **solve a simpler problem**.
- Use play money.

Strategies

- **Make a chart.**
- **Use a model.**
- **Draw a picture.**
- **Solve a simpler problem.**
- **Work backward.**
- **Guess and test.**
- **Make an organized list.**
- **Use a pattern.**

Record the different ways to make 5¢.
Record all the different ways
to make 10¢, then 15¢, then 20¢.
Use a chart to record each way.
How many different ways can you make 20¢?

How could you have solved this problem
another way?

Practice

Choose one of the **Strategies**

1. Show 4 ways you could make 55¢ with 6 or
   fewer coins.

2. The pizzas in Tony's Restaurant have these toppings:
   pepperoni, mushroom, and green pepper.
   You can choose 1, 2, or 3 toppings.
   How many different pizzas can you make?

3. What number am I?
   • I have 2 digits.
   • I am less than 90.
   • I am more than 20.
   • My ones digit is 1 more than my tens digit.
   How many numbers did you find?

Reflect

Tell about a time when you had to buy something with coins.
How did you decide which coins to use?

LESSON

1

1. **a)** Ask your classmates:
   Are you left-handed, right-handed, or both?
   Record the data in a tally chart.
   b) Tell 3 things your chart shows.

2. **a)** Ask your classmates to name their favourite TV show.
   Record the data in a list.
   b) Ask a question about your data.
   Answer the question.
   c) Why might someone want to know about these data?

3. **a)** Measure the distance from wrist to shoulder on 5 classmates.
   Record the measurements in a chart.
   b) How well do you think the chart shows this data?
   Explain.

2

4. Emily made this line plot
   to record the items she sold
   at a craft sale.
   a) How many items did
   Emily sell altogether?
   b) Suppose Emily sold 1 more
   bracelet and 1 less basket.
   How would the line plot
   change?

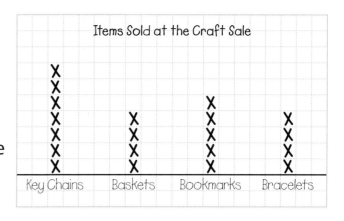

3

5. Children in Grade 3 read about the medals Canada won at the Winter Olympics in 2006.
  a) Did Canada win more silver or bronze medals? How many more?
  b) How many medals did Canada win altogether at these games?
  c) Write 2 other things you know from the graph.

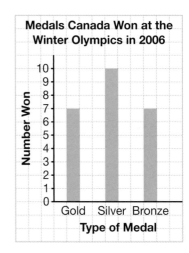

Medals Canada Won at the Winter Olympics in 2006

4

6. Ty used tally marks to show the number of stamps in his collection.
  a) Draw a bar graph to show the data.
  b) Ty wants 1 page in his album to have all the stamps from 2 countries.
    He wants 16 stamps on this page.
    From which countries should Ty choose the stamps?
  c) Why do you think Ty used "Other"?

Stamp Collection	
France	|||||	
Spain	|||||
Mexico	||||| |||||
Sweden	||||| |||
Other	|||

3
4

7. a) Draw a different bar graph to show the data in question 6.
  b) How are the bar graphs the same?

5

8. Choose a chart, list, line plot, or graph from this unit.
  a) Write a problem you can solve with the data.
  b) Solve the problem.
    Tell about your solution.

UNIT
7 Learning Goals

☑ collect and organize data
☑ use tally marks, charts, lists, and line plots
☑ read bar graphs
☑ draw bar graphs
☑ use bar graphs to solve problems

At the Vet

Veterinarians record data about animals.

Part 1

➤ Ask your classmates to name their favourite farm animal.
➤ Collect the data in a tally chart or line plot.
➤ Tell how you organized the data.
➤ Write 3 things you know from your data.

Part 2

Use the bar graph.

➤ Which 2 types of animals did the vet see the same number of times? How do you know?
➤ How many animals did the vet see altogether?
➤ Write a question about the bar graph. Answer your question.

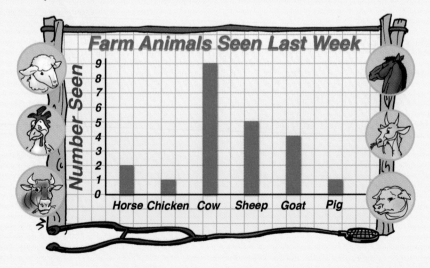

Farm Animals Seen Last Week

Part 3

Make up a problem about a vet or about farm animals.
➤ Write a question that can help you solve your problem.
➤ Collect and organize the data.
➤ Show the data in a bar graph.
➤ Solve the problem.
➤ How did you use the graph to solve the problem?

Problem Topics
- a visit to the open house at a vet's clinic
- a day travelling to farms with a vet
- unusual farm animals
- a bison farm

Reflect on Your Learning

What have you learned about collecting and organizing data?

Multiplication

Sports Day

Learning Goals

- model multiplication and division up to 5 × 5
- find strategies to multiply and divide up to 5 × 5
- pose and solve story problems involving multiplication and division

and Division

Key Words

. . . .

multiply

multiplication sentence

times

equal groups

array

product

divide

division sentence

divided by

The school is planning a Sports Day.
The grade 3 class will get the equipment ready.

How many pylons are there?
How many basketballs?
How could you find out without counting each one?

Investigating Equal Groups

Yvan went to Jasper National Park with
his family.
As they drove, he saw some mountain goats.
Yvan had only a few seconds to count
the goats.

How can you find the number of goats without
counting each one?

Explore

Game

You will need 5 sets of dot cards
with 1 to 5 dots on each.

➤ Player 1, cover your eyes.
➤ Player 2,
  • select 2 to 5 cards with
    the same number of dots.
  • Place the cards face up on
    the table.
  • Ask your partner to open
    his eyes and tell how many
    dots there are.
➤ Take turns to repeat the activity.

Show and Share

What strategies did you use to count the dots?
How can you find the total number of dots without
counting each one?

Equal groups have the same number of things in each group.

These beads come in packages of 5.

How many beads are in 3 packages?

Use equal groups to find how many.

➤ Draw the 3 packages. Show the number of beads in each package.

➤ Skip count to find the total number of beads. There are 15 beads in all.

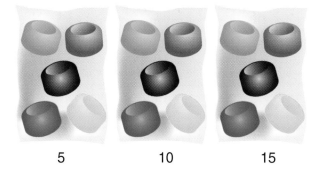

5   10   15

We write "3 groups of 5 equals 15" as a **multiplication sentence.**

3   ×   5   =   15

| Number of groups | Number of things in each group | Total number of things The **product** |

We say, "3 **times** 5 equals 15."

I can show multiplication in different ways.

: : :

3 groups of 2 is 6.

3 X 2 = 6

Practice

1. Use dot cards or make a picture to show each set.
   a) 2 groups of 5
   b) 2 groups of 4
   c) 2 groups of 2
   d) 1 group of 5

2. Write a multiplication sentence for each picture.

   a)

   b)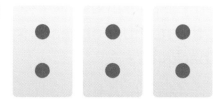

   c)

   d)

3. Tennis balls come in packages of 3.
   The gym teacher brought 3 packages
   for her class.
   How many tennis balls did she bring?
   Draw a picture and write a number sentence
   to show your solution.

4. Draw a picture to show the product of 3 × 4.
   Write a story problem to go with your picture.

5. Find each product.
   a) 4 × 2   b) 3 × 4
   c) 1 × 3   d) 5 × 1
   e) 2 × 5   f) 4 × 5

6. Multiply.
   a) 1 × 4   b) 3 × 3
   c) 2 × 3   d) 4 × 3
   e) 1 × 5   f) 5 × 2

7. For which pictures can you write a multiplication sentence?
Write the multiplication sentence when it is possible.
If you cannot write a multiplication sentence, use words,
pictures, or numbers to show why not.

a)

b)

c)

d)

8. a) Kayla uses straws and pipe cleaners
to make triangles.
She must not bend the straws.
How many straws will Kayla
need to make 4 triangles?

b) Suppose Kayla makes 4 squares.
Will she need more or fewer straws?
How do you know?

9. Can you write a multiplication sentence for this picture?
Explain why or why not.

Reflect

When can you use a multiplication
sentence to find how many?
Use words, pictures, or
numbers to explain.

At Home

Find 3 things at home that
come in equal groups.
How many will there be
in 2 groups? 3 groups?

Closest to Twelve

You will need 75 counters and 4 sets of cards numbered 1 to 5. The object of the game is to get an answer closest to 12.

➤ Shuffle the cards and place them face down in a pile.

➤ Turn over the top card. Place it beside the pile. This card tells the number of groups of counters.

➤ Each player takes a card from the pile. This card tells the number of counters in each group.

➤ Take the counters you need. Write a multiplication sentence that shows how many counters you took.

➤ The player with the answer closest to 12 gets a point.

➤ If more than one player has an answer closest to 12, no one gets a point.

➤ The first player to get 5 points is the winner.

Relating Multiplication and Repeated Addition

Explore

Keera walks 4 blocks every school day.
She adds each daily distance to find her
weekly total.
How many blocks in all would she walk
- by Monday?
- by Tuesday?
- by Friday?

Record your work in pictures and in numbers.

Show and Share

Share your work with a classmate.
How can you use addition to solve the problem?
How can you use multiplication?

Connect

You can use **repeated addition** to think about multiplication.

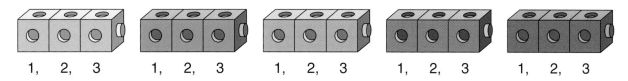

1, 2, 3   1, 2, 3   1, 2, 3   1, 2, 3   1, 2, 3

Join the Snap Cubes to make a long train.

$$3 + 3 + 3 + 3 + 3 = 15$$
$$5 \times 3 = 15$$

A **number line** can also show
multiplication as repeated addition.

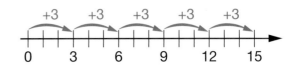

Add 3 each time.
5 "times" 3 equals 15.

Practice

1. Show each repeated addition using Snap Cubes.
   Write a multiplication sentence for each addition sentence.
   a) $1 + 1 + 1 + 1 = 4$
   b) $5 + 5 = 10$
   c) $4 + 4 + 4 + 4 + 4 = 20$
   d) $0 + 0 + 0 = 0$

2. Write an addition sentence for each multiplication sentence.
   Draw a picture to show the result.
   a) $2 \times 3 = 6$ b) $5 \times 1 = 5$ c) $4 \times 3 = 12$

3. For each picture, write an addition sentence and
   a multiplication sentence.
   a) How many tickets do the
      children need?

   b) How many toys fit
      on the shelves?

4. Ken says you cannot use repeated addition for 1×5.
   Do you agree? Use words, pictures, or numbers to explain.

5. Karla made a bead necklace to sell
   at the craft fair.
   She used 4 sets of beads like this.
   How many beads did Karla use?

   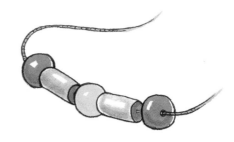

6. Sia read the same number of books each school day this week. How many books did she read in all if she read

   a) 1 book each day?
   b) 2 books each day?
   c) 3 books each day?
   d) 4 books each day?
   e) 5 books each day?

   What patterns do you notice?

7. Write an addition sentence and a multiplication sentence for each number line.

   a)
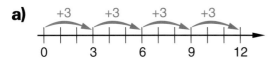

   b)
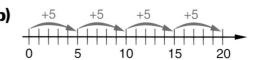

8. Karen and 3 of her friends are hoop dancers.
   Each dancer uses 5 hoops for a special dance.
   How many hoops are used in all?
   Show your answer using pictures, words, or numbers.

9. Create a story problem for each question.
   Solve each problem using words, pictures, and numbers.
   a) 3×3 **b)** $5 + 5 + 5$ **c)** 2×5 **d)** $1 + 1 + 1 + 1$

10. Draw a picture for each question.
   Write the number sentence for each.
   How are the 2 number sentences the same?
   How are they different?
   a) Add: 4 and 5
   b) Multiply: 4 and 5

Reflect

When can you use multiplication as a shortcut for adding?
When can you not?

Using Arrays to Multiply

Jesse's class is raising money for hunger relief.
The children are making pompom people to sell.
They have different size boxes.
They want to pack the pompom people in equal rows in the boxes.

Explore

You will need 25 counters for each pair.

➤ Find ways to pack up to 25 pompom people in equal rows. Use counters to show each way.

➤ Record each way you find.
  • Tell the number of rows.
  • Tell the number of pompom people in each row.
  • Tell the number of pompom people that will fit in the box.

Show *and* Share

Share your answers with another pair of classmates.
See if they found any answers different from yours.

An **array** is an arrangement of objects in equal rows.

This is a 4-by-3 array.
There are 4 equal rows with
3 counters in each row.
$4 \times 3 = 12$

This is a 2-by-2 array.
There are 2 equal rows with
2 counters in each row.
$2 \times 2 = 4$

This is a 1-by-4 array.
There is 1 row with
4 counters in the row.
$1 \times 4 = 4$

We know that we can think of multiplication as repeated addition.

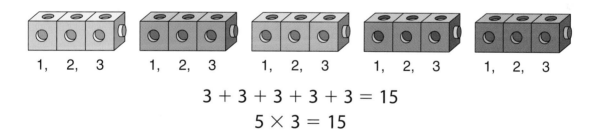

1, 2, 3   1, 2, 3   1, 2, 3   1, 2, 3   1, 2, 3

$$3 + 3 + 3 + 3 + 3 = 15$$
$$5 \times 3 = 15$$

We can arrange these Snap Cubes to make an array.

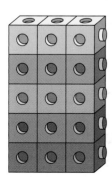

This is a 5-by-3 array.
There are 5 equal rows with
3 Snap Cubes in each row.
$5 \times 3 = 15$

1. Write a multiplication sentence for each array.

   a)

   b)

   c)

   d)

2. There are 20 desks in a classroom.
   The teacher wants to move the desks
   from small groups into rows.
   He wants the same number of desks in each row.
   Write multiplication sentences to show
   how the desks could be arranged.

3. Sergio wants to grow tomato plants in his garden.
   He puts 5 plants in each row.
   How many rows does he need to plant
   to have at least 12 plants?

4. Use grid paper or counters to make an array for each sentence.
   a) $1 \times 1 = 1$ **b)** $2 \times 2 = 4$ **c)** $3 \times 3 = 9$
   d) $4 \times 4 = 16$ **e)** $5 \times 5 = 25$
   What do you notice about the shape of each array? Explain.

5. Use counters or grid paper.
   Make an array to find each product.
   a) 2×3 **b)** 4×3 **c)** 3×5
   d) 3×4 **e)** 5×1 **f)** 2×4
   g) 2×5 **h)** 3×2 **i)** 4×1

6. Write a multiplication sentence for each picture.
Explain your thinking.

   a) How many tiles are in the whole patio?

   b) How many pieces are in the whole puzzle?

7. **a)** Bakers use arrays to count the cookies in each batch.
Write a multiplication sentence for each tray of cookies.

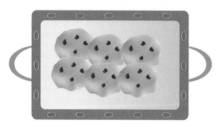 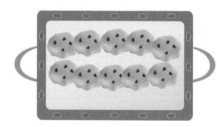

   b) The baker decided to make more cookies.
He doubled the number of rows on each tray.
What happened to the number of cookies?
Will this always happen? Explain.

8. Make up a multiplication problem about something in an array.
Trade problems with a classmate. Solve the problem.

Reflect

How is using arrays to multiply like using equal groups?
How is it different?

Relating Multiplication Sentences

Explore . . . .

You will need scissors and sheets of 4-by-4 grid paper.
Use the grid paper to draw as many different arrays as you can.
Cut out each array.
Write a multiplication sentence on each array.
Look for arrays with the same shape and size.
What do you notice?

Show *and* Share

Share your arrays with another pair of classmates.
Look for arrays that have the same product but different
multiplication sentences. What do you notice?
Why do you think that happens?

Connect . . . .

Kim used 5-by-5 grids to make arrays.
Here are 2 matching arrays that Kim made.

| 4 rows of 5 | Turn the | 5 rows of 4 |
| $4 \times 5 = 20$ | array on its side. | $5 \times 4 = 20$ |

When you **multiply** 2 numbers, you can switch the order
of the numbers without changing the product.

We can show the same idea using **equal groups**.

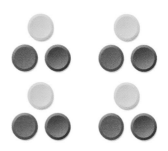

3 groups of 4
$3 \times 4 = 12$

4 groups of 3
$4 \times 3 = 12$

When we switch the *number of groups* and the *number of objects in each group*, we still have the same total number of objects. So, the product is the same.

Practice

1. Write 2 multiplication sentences for each array.

   a)

   b)

2. Arrange each set into an array with at least 2 rows and 2 columns.
   Make a drawing to show your thinking.
   Write 2 multiplication sentences and 2 repeated addition sentences for each array.

   a)

   b)

   c)

3. How can you show that 2 bags of 5 marbles and 5 bags of 2 marbles contain the same number of marbles?
Use words, pictures, and numbers to explain your thinking.

4. a) Make 2 arrays that each have only 1 multiplication sentence. Record your arrays.

b) Describe why you can write only 1 multiplication sentence for the arrays you made.

5. Cover Me!

You will need
- a 10-by-10 grid,
- 2-colour counters, and
- 4 sets of cards numbered 1 to 5.

Start by choosing your colour of counter.

➤ Shuffle the cards and place them face down.

➤ Each player takes 2 cards from the top of the deck.

➤ Player 1 uses counters to make an array anywhere on the grid, to match the numbers showing on his cards.

➤ Player 2 uses counters to make an array to match her cards. You cannot put a counter on a square that is already covered!

➤ Players find the products for their arrays. The product tells you your score for that turn.

➤ Play again. Continue until both players cannot fit an array on the grid.

➤ Add your points. The player with the most points wins.

Reflect

Suppose you have to multiply 2 numbers.
Tell 3 different strategies you can use to find the product.

Division as Grouping

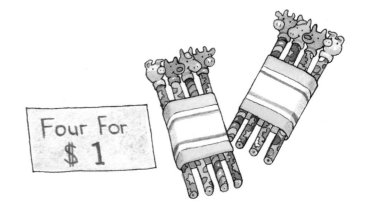

Four For $1

Many things come in equal groups.
Where have you seen things in
equal groups?

Explore

You will need up to 20 blocks.

Ani is making grab bags for a garage sale.
She wants to put the same number
of toys in each bag.
Help her plan ways to package the toys.

➤ Choose 8 blocks.
  Put the blocks into groups so there
  is the same number in each group.
  How many bags would Ani need?

➤ Repeat the activity with 15 blocks.

➤ Repeat with a number that you choose.

➤ Record your work.

Show *and* Share

Share your answers with a classmate.
Tell how you made equal groups.
Could you always make equal groups? Why or why not?

Division can be used to find how many equal groups there are when you know the size of the groups.

➤ Start with 12 counters.

➤ **Divide** the 12 counters into groups of 3. Count the number of groups.

I count out 3. Then I start a new group.

➤ Write the **division sentence.**

12	÷	3	=	4
↑		↑		↑
Number of counters		Number in each group		Number of groups

We say, "12 **divided by** 3 equals 4."

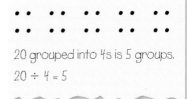

20 grouped into 4s is 5 groups.
20 ÷ 4 = 5

I can show division in different ways.

1. Use blocks. Find the number of groups.
Write a division sentence for each problem.
   a) Divide 6 blocks into groups of 2.
   b) Divide 8 blocks into groups of 4.
   c) Divide 12 blocks into groups of 4.

2. Draw a picture and write a number sentence
to solve each problem.

   a) Each room has 4 beds.
   How many rooms are needed
   for 20 children?

   b) Each all-terrain vehicle
   has 3 wheels.
   How many all-terrain vehicles
   can be made with 15 wheels?

3. Use blocks. Make equal groups to divide.
   a) $12 \div 4$ **b)** $10 \div 5$ **c)** $8 \div 2$
   d) $15 \div 3$ **e)** $6 \div 2$ **f)** $10 \div 1$
   g) $4 \div 2$ **h)** $8 \div 4$ **i)** $6 \div 3$

4. Terry's class is ordering extra-long
submarine sandwiches for a party.
Each submarine sandwich can feed 4 children.
How many submarine sandwiches do
they need to feed 16 children?

5. Zachary wanted to put 3 ice cubes into 3 glasses.
When he opened the cooler, all the ice cubes were gone.
Write a division sentence.
Explain what will always happen when 0 is divided
into equal groups.

6. Omar has 20 photos to put in an album. He has 5 blank pages.
He wants to put the same number of photos on each page.
How many photos might Omar put on each page?

7. The grade 3 classes are going on a field trip to a lake.
Create at least 2 division problems from the picture.
Solve the problems.

Reflect

Think about division as making equal groups.
What does each number in this division sentence represent?
$9 \div 3 = 3$
Use words, pictures, or numbers to explain your thinking.

Division as Sharing

What card games do you know?
Some games start by giving each person the same number of cards.

Explore

Antoine knows a game that starts with 15 number cards.
How can Antoine share the 15 cards equally among 3 players?
➤ Show a way using materials.
➤ Record your way using pictures, words, and numbers.
➤ Now find a way to share the 15 cards equally among 5 players.
Record your way.

Show and Share

Share your answers with another pair of classmates.
What strategies did you use to share the cards equally?

Connect

Division can be used to find how many are in each group when you know the number of groups.

Four children helped clean the classroom. The teacher has 12 stickers to share equally among the 4 children as a reward.

The teacher puts the 12 stickers, one by one, into 4 piles until all the stickers are gone.

- 1 sticker in each pile

- 2 stickers in each pile

- 3 stickers in each pile

We can say, "12 shared equally into 4 groups is 3 in each group."
Write the division sentence.

12   ÷   4   =   3
↑   ↑   ↑

Number of   Number of   Number of stickers
stickers   groups   in each group

We say, "12 divided by 4 equals 3."

Practice

Use materials to model the problems.

1. Find the number of objects in each group.
   Write a division sentence to record your work.

   a) 8 hockey sticks
   are divided into
   2 equal groups.

   b) 25 marbles
   are divided into
   5 equal groups.

   c) 9 balls
   are divided into
   3 equal groups.

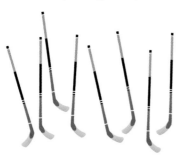  

2. The teacher put the desks into 4 equal groups.
There are 20 desks in the classroom.
How many desks are in each group?

3. Kim divided 25 markers into 5 equal piles.
How many markers are in each pile?

4. Find the number of things in each group.
   a) 15 ÷ 5   **b)** 12 ÷ 4   **c)** 6 ÷ 3
   d) 8 ÷ 2   **e)** 9 ÷ 3   **f)** 10 ÷ 5
   g) 4 ÷ 2   **h)** 10 ÷ 2   **i)** 8 ÷ 4

5. The camp leader took 10 children
on a scavenger hunt.
She divided the children into equal teams.
How many children might have been
on each team?
Show how you solved the problem.

6. Create an equal sharing problem for each
division question below.
Show how to solve the problem using pictures,
words, or numbers.
   a) 9 ÷ 3   **b)** 15 ÷ 5   **c)** 10 ÷ 2   **d)** 25 ÷ 5

Math Link

Measurement

Cut a strip of paper that is 12 cm long. Fold it
in half twice to make 4 equal pieces.
How long is each piece?
How is your paper folding related to division?

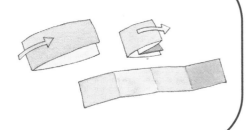

Reflect

What are 2 ways to think about division?
Use examples to explain.

Relating Division and Repeated Subtraction

Jéanne has 8 photos from her school picnic.
She wants to give 2 photos to each of her friends.
How many friends will get 2 photos before she runs out?

➤ Choose materials to model the problem.
  Draw a picture to show your solution.

➤ Suppose Jéanne had 10 photos.
  How many friends would get 2 photos?

Show *and* Share

Share your answers with another pair of classmates.
How do your pictures remind you of division?

Connect

Sophie and Alex use repeated subtraction to find 6 ÷ 2.

➤ Sophie counts how many groups of 2 she
  has to subtract until no items remain.

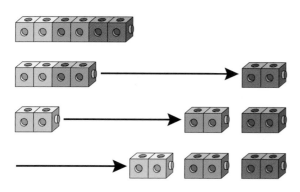

6 subtract 2 is 4, subtract 2 more is 2, and subtract 2 more is 0. That's 3 groups.

➤ Alex puts the 6 items into 2 equal groups, then counts.

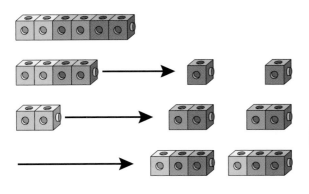

6 subtract 2 is
1 in each group,
subtract 2 more is
2 in each group, and
subtract 2 more is
3 in each group.

➤ A number line can also show how division is like repeated subtraction.

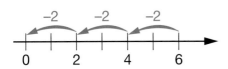

Start at 6. Subtract 2 each time until you reach 0.
$6 - 2 - 2 - 2 = 0$
Count the number of jumps to get from 6 to 0.
$6 \div 2 = 3$

Practice

1. Write a division sentence for each repeated subtraction sentence.

a) $4 - 1 - 1 - 1 - 1 = 0$

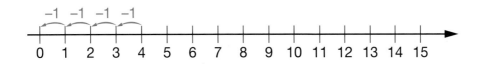

b) $12 - 4 - 4 - 4 = 0$

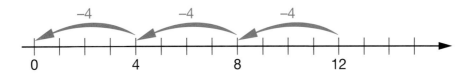

c) $8 - 4 - 4 = 0$

each division sentence as repeated subtraction.
e repeated subtraction in a picture.

= 5   **b)** 10 ÷ 2 = 5   **c)** 5 ÷ 5 = 1

ina's CD player uses 2 batteries.
she has a pack of 8 batteries.
How many times can Brianna change
the batteries?

4. Jason delivers 15 newspapers every
Saturday morning.
He can deliver 3 newspapers every minute.
How long does it take Jason to deliver
all 15 newspapers?

5. Kaytlyn gave out stickers as prizes at the school fair.
After each game, Kaytlyn gave 1 sticker
to each child who placed first, second, and third.
The stickers came in strips of 12.
How many games were played before the stickers ran out?

6. Write your own division problem.
Trade problems with a classmate.
Show how you would solve your classmate's problem.

7. How is 8 − 2 different from 8 ÷ 2?
Show your thinking using pictures, words, or numbers.

 **Math** **Link**

Money

Suppose you wanted something that costs 20¢.
To find how many nickels are in 20¢, divide by 5.
What division statement can you write to show
the number of pennies in 5¢?

8. Nathan visited the Athabasca Glacier
when he was 7 years old.
He learned that the glacier melts
3 m every year.

Nathan returned to see the glacier
when he was older.
He learned it had melted 15 m
since his first visit.
How many years had it been since
his first visit?

Athabasca is the Cree name for
"where there are reeds."

9. Leila and Leo enjoy the rides at the Calgary Stampede.
They can buy ride tickets in strips of 10, 15, or 20.

a) Leila likes the motorcycle ride.
How many rides can she have with each strip of tickets?
Which strip of tickets will be completely used up?
How do you know?

b) Leo likes the Ferris wheel.
How many rides can he have with each strip of tickets?

Reflect

How can repeated subtraction help you divide?
Use an example to explain.

Relating Multiplication and Division Using Arrays

You will need counters and a copy of the picture below.

Zachary's school is going to a concert.
The teachers are buying tickets in the blue seats.

Class	Number of People
Grade 1A	16
Grade 1B	15
Grade 2A	15
Grade 2B	15
Grade 3A	20
Grade 3B	25

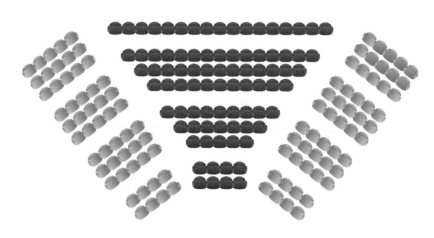

Find a way to fit everybody in the blue seats.
Try to keep the people in each class together.
Record your plan.

Show *and* Share

Share your work with another pair of classmates.
How could multiplication help you complete your
seating plan?
How could division help you decide the number
of rows for each class?

An array can show multiplication.

3 rows of 4
$3 \times 4 = 12$

4 rows of 3
$4 \times 3 = 12$

An array can also show division.

12 objects in all

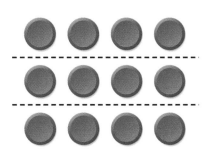

12 divided into
3 groups
$12 \div 3 = 4$

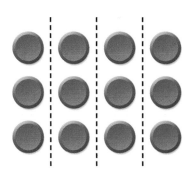

12 divided into
4 groups
$12 \div 4 = 3$

$3 \times 4 = 12$
$4 \times 3 = 12$
$12 \div 3 = 4$
$12 \div 4 = 3$

These *multiplication* and
division sentences
are **related sentences**.

...tion sentence for each picture.
...sentence for each picture.

b)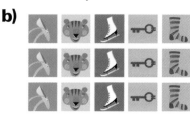
c)

2. Use counters to make an array for each number.
   For each array, write 2 multiplication sentences
   and 2 division sentences.
   a) 12   **b)** 8   **c)** 6

3. Divide. How can you use multiplication to help you?
   a) $9 \div 3$ **b)** $15 \div 3$ **c)** $20 \div 4$ **d)** $4 \div 4$
   e) $10 \div 5$ **f)** $25 \div 5$ **g)** $6 \div 3$ **h)** $5 \div 1$

For questions 4 and 5, show your work using pictures,
words, or numbers.

4. Lydia is putting her collection of hockey cards
   into an album.
   Each page can hold 12 cards.
   Each page has 4 rows of pockets.
   How many cards can go in each row?

5. How can you use an array to multiply?
   How can you use an array to divide?
   Explain using words, pictures, and
   number sentences.

Reflect

How can multiplication help you understand division?

Relating Multiplication and Division Using Groups

In art class, the Grade 3 students learned how to make beads out of paper. Suppose you are helping to organize the beads to sell at a school fair. What do you know about counting collections that could help you?

Explore

You will need 50 counters and 2 sets of cards numbered 1 to 5.

➤ Each partner selects 2 cards without looking.
  • Card 1 tells the number of groups of counters.
  • Card 2 tells the number of counters in each group.
  Take that many counters and put them in a pile.
  Write a multiplication sentence to show how many counters you took.

➤ Switch piles with your partner.
  Find ways to make equal groups with the counters.
  Write a division sentence for each way you find.

➤ Share your multiplication and division sentences.
  What do you notice?

Replace the counters and the cards. Repeat the activity.

Show and Share

Share your work with another pair of classmates.
Talk about any patterns you see.

...vision are related.

$2 \times 5 = \mathbf{10}$

You need to find:
- the number of objects in all

...ber of groups
number of objects
in each group

Division as Grouping

You know:
- the number of objects in each group
- the number of objects in all

$10 \div 5 = \mathbf{2}$

You need to find:
- the number of groups

Division as Sharing

You know:
- the number of objects in all
- the number of groups

$10 \div 2 = \mathbf{5}$

You need to find:
- the number of objects in each group

Sometimes multiplication can help you think about division.
What is $20 \div 4$?

$4 \times \square = 20$
You know $4 \times \mathbf{5} = 20$.
So, $20 \div 4 = 5$.

 Think: 4 times which number is 20?

Practice

1. Write a multiplication and a division problem for each picture.

   a)

   b)

   c)

2. Tao bought some packs of collector cards.
   Each pack holds 5 cards. There are 25 cards altogether.
   How many packs did he buy?

3. Write the related number sentences for each set of numbers.
   a) 3, 5, 15   b) 4, 2, 8
   c) 2, 5, 10   d) 4, 3, 12
   e) 5, 5, 25   f) 4, 5, 20

4. Sean bought 4 submarine sandwiches.
   He cut each sandwich into 3 pieces.
   Then Sean and his 2 friends shared
   the sandwiches equally.
   How many pieces did each person get?

5. Dana's dog is 20 kg. It is 4 times as heavy
   as it was as a puppy. What was the mass
   of Dana's dog when it was a puppy?

6. Samuel walks 8 blocks to school each day.
   Samuel walks 4 times as far to school as
   his friend Craig.
   How many blocks does Craig walk to school?

7. Make up a multiplication and division problem
   for each set of numbers.
   a) 4, 2, 2   b) 15, 3, 5   c) 10, 2, 5

8. Explain what each of the numbers 4, 3, and 12
   could mean in these related number sentences.
   $4 \times 3 = 12$ $3 \times 4 = 12$
   $12 \div 4 = 3$ $12 \div 3 = 4$

Reflect

Show 3 different ways to find $15 \div 3$.
Use words, numbers, or pictures to explain each way.

Strategies Toolkit

Explore

● ●

Karlee has 3 T-shirts and 2 pairs of pants.
How many different outfits can
Karlee make? Show your work.

Show and Share

Show how you found the outfits.
Explain your strategy.

Connect

● ● ● ● ● ● ● ● ● ● ● ● ● ● ● ● ● ● ● ●

Ben is getting a new bike. He can choose
a racing bike, a mountain bike, or a BMX bike.
Each bike comes in blue, black, silver, or red.
How many different bikes can Ben choose?

Strategies

- **Make a chart.**
- **Use a model.**
- **Draw a picture.**
- **Solve a simpler problem.**
- **Work backward.**
- **Guess and test.**
- **Make an organized list.**
- **Use a pattern.**

Understand

What do you know?
- There are 3 different bikes.
- There are 4 different colours.
- You want to find how many
  different bikes are possible.

Plan

Think of a strategy to help you
solve the problem.
- You could **make a chart**.
- Here are the bikes that are blue.
  Copy and complete the chart
  for each of the other colours.

Colour	Bike
blue	racing
blue	mountain
blue	BMX

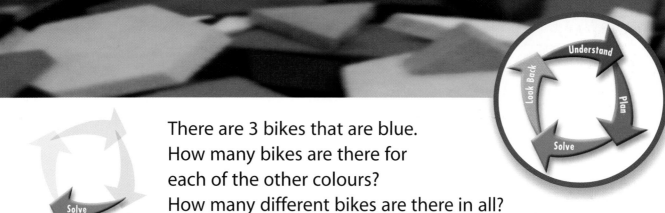

There are 3 bikes that are blue.
How many bikes are there for
each of the other colours?
How many different bikes are there in all?

How can multiplication help you to
solve the problem?

Practice

Choose one of the

Strategies

1. Zakia will pack 1 game and 1 toy for her
   overnight stay with her aunt.
   • For the game, she will choose either
     checkers or cards.
   • For the toy, she will choose a truck, a bear,
     a rabbit, or a hula hoop.
   How many choices does Zakia have?

2. Make a plan for a school break day in the day-care centre.
   Children can choose 1 outside activity and 1 afternoon movie.
   List up to 4 choices for the outside activity.
   List up to 4 choices for the movie.
   How many choices will the children have?

Reflect

How does making a chart help to solve a problem?
Can you solve the problem without completing the chart?
Explain.

1

1. Multiply.
   a) 3×2 **b)** 4×1 **c)** 1×3 **d)** 5×5
   e) 4×5 **f)** 2×4 **g)** 2×1 **h)** 5×1

2. Draw a picture for each answer.
   a) Find 2 ways to make equal teams from 8 children.
   b) Find 2 ways to make equal teams from 10 children.

2

3. Design an Inukshuk with Pattern Blocks.
   Suppose you want to make 3 Inukshuks.
   How many of each type of block do you need?
   Write a repeated addition and a multiplication sentence for each answer.

3

4. Draw arrays for the following multiplication sentences:
   a) $3 \times 1 = 3$ **b)** $4 \times 1 = 4$ **c)** $5 \times 1 = 5$
   $\ 3 \times 2 = 6$ $\ 4 \times 2 = 8$ $\ 5 \times 2 = 10$
   $\ 3 \times 3 = 9$ $\ 4 \times 3 = 12$ $\ 5 \times 3 = 15$
   What patterns do you notice? Why are they happening?
   Write the next 2 multiplication sentences in each set.

4

5. Nadine found that $2 \times 5 = 10$ and $5 \times 2 = 10$.
   She wonders why the answers are the same.
   Use pictures, numbers, and words to show why.

5

6. Write a list of 3 things that come in equal groups of 5 or less.
   Write a division problem for each. Solve each problem.

7. Use counters. Find the number of counters in each group.
   a) $9 \div 3$ **b)** $16 \div 4$ **c)** $12 \div 3$
   d) $20 \div 4$ **e)** $6 \div 2$ **f)** $8 \div 4$

8. How could these cards be shared equally among 4 children? Explain using pictures and a number sentence.

9. Tao has 20 tokens to play either *Basketball* or *Skee Ball*. Use repeated subtraction and division to show how many times Tao could play each game.

10. Write multiplication sentences that can help you solve the division problems.
  a) $12 \div 3 = \square$ **b)** $16 \div 4 = \square$
  Draw an array to show how the sentences are related.

11. Write related facts for each set of numbers.
  a) 2, 4, 8   **b)** 3, 5, 15
  c) 4, 3, 12   **d)** 5, 5, 25

12. Write division sentences that are related to the multiplication sentences.
  a) $3 \times 3 = 9$ **b)** $5 \times 4 = 20$

UNIT

8 Learning Goals

☑ model multiplication and division up to 5×5
☑ find strategies to multiply and divide up to 5×5
☑ pose and solve story problems involving multiplication and division

Unit Problem

Sports Day

The group leaders need to make equal teams for each Sports Day activity.

Part 1

Organize each class into equal teams, with at least 3 children on a team.

Show your work using pictures, numbers, or words.

Kindergarten	12 children
Grade 1	15 children
Grade 2	20 children
Grade 3	16 children
Grade 4	25 children

Activity 1: Basketball Throw

Part 2

Pick a Sports Day activity.
Make up a multiplication problem for the activity.
Show how you would solve your problem.
Think of a division problem related to your multiplication problem.
Show how you would solve your problem.

Activity 2: Freeze Tag

Check List

Your work should show

☑ how you organized the classes into equal teams

☑ the multiplication problem you made

☑ the division problem you made

☑ clear explanations of how to solve your problems

Activity 3: Ping Pong Throw

Reflect on Your Learning

What do you know about multiplication and division that you did not know before? Describe your ideas using pictures, numbers, and words.

Investigation

Are You a Square or a Rectangle?

Part 1

You will need a measuring tape.

➤ Measure your partner's height with her shoes off.
➤ Measure her arm span.
➤ Record these measurements in a chart.

Height	Arm Span

➤ Have your partner take the same measurements from you. Compare your height and your arm span.
  • If your height is greater than your arm span, you are a tall rectangle.
  • If your height is less than your arm span, you are a short rectangle.
  • If your height and arm span are within 2 cm, you are a square.

Are you a tall rectangle, a short rectangle, or a square?

Tall rectangle

Short rectangle

Square

Part 2

You will need grid paper.

➤ Collect data from your classmates.
  Have each student record his shape on
  a tally chart or line plot.
  • Which shape is most common?
    Least common?

➤ Draw a bar graph to show the data.
  Compare your graph with those of other
  classmates.
  How are the graphs the same? Different?

➤ Write your own question about the graph.
  Answer your question.

Display Your Work

Record your findings using words, pictures, or numbers.

Take It Further

Find the shapes of friends and family members.
How do their shapes compare with your classmates' shapes?
Write about what you find out.

UNIT

1

1. **a)** Make a pattern that starts with 1 ⬜, and adds more ⬜s each time.
   b) Show your pattern in a picture.
   c) Write the pattern rule.

2. What is the pattern rule?
   Copy the pattern to fill in the missing numbers.
   a) 24, 27, ___, ___, 36, 39, ___
   b) 87, 77, ___, 57, ___, ___, 27

3. **a)** Make a pattern that starts with 15 ⬜s, and removes some ⬜s each time.
   b) Show your pattern in a picture.
   c) Write the pattern rule.

2

4. Use the digits 5, 9, and 7. Use each digit once.
   a) Write as many 3-digit numbers as you can.
   b) Order the numbers from least to greatest.
   c) Which of your numbers is the greatest? The least?

5. Start at 350. Count on by 25s to 900.
   Write each number as you count.
   What patterns do you see in the ones digits?
   The tens digits? The hundreds digits?

6. Find 3 different ways to make two dollars and twenty-eight cents, using pennies, dimes, and loonies.

3

7. 9, 5, and ⬜ are the numbers in a set of related facts.
   a) What could the missing number be?
   Write the related facts.
   b) What is another possible missing number?
   Write the related facts for this number.

8. Find each missing number. Explain your strategy.
   a) $3 + \square = 8$
   b) $16 - \square = 7$
   c) $\square + 3 = 14$

9. Add or subtract. Show your strategy.
   a) 138 + 722   b) 427 + 299   c) 291 + 305
   d) 495 − 303   e) 400 − 105   f) 757 − 238

10. Five hundred sixty-seven children
    are at track and field day.
    • 163 are in track events only.
    • 139 are in field events only.
    • All the others are in the stands.
    Make a story problem about
    track and field day.
    Solve your problem. Show your work.

11. Jan is planning a trip with her family.
    They plan to leave on July 7.
    They plan to come home on August 3.
    How many days will their trip last?

12. Use a ruler. Draw a line that is
    a) 14 cm long
    b) 5 cm long
    c) 23 cm long

13. You will need a ruler and a book.
    Find the perimeter of the book cover.

14. Which unit would you use to measure the mass of each object,
    grams or kilograms?
    a)    b)    c)    d)

15. Draw a picture to show each fraction.
   a) 2 fourths of a pie
   b) 3 eighths of a pie
   c) 5 eighths of a pie

16. Make a story about one of your pictures from question 15.

17. Which fraction in each pair is greater? Use pictures, words, or numbers to explain your thinking.
   a) $\frac{1}{3}$ and $\frac{2}{3}$ **b)** $\frac{1}{4}$ and $\frac{4}{4}$
   c) $\frac{7}{8}$ and $\frac{3}{8}$ **d)** $\frac{5}{9}$ and $\frac{2}{9}$

6

18. Name each polygon you see in this picture.

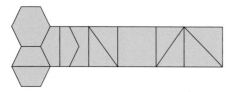

   Write the name of each polygon.
   Write the number of sides.

19. **a)** Which objects below are prisms?
           Explain your thinking.
       b) Which objects are pyramids?
           Explain your thinking.

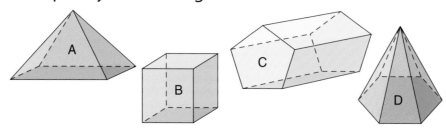

20. Use the objects in question 19. Name each object.
For each object, tell the number of faces, edges, and vertices.

7

21. Amira asked some friends to spell their names.
She listed the number of letters in each name.
3, 5, 4, 7, 5, 4, 6, 4, 3, 7, 5, 5, 3, 8, 7, 5, 6, 3
a) Show the data in a line plot.
b) Write a question that you can answer from the line plot.
Answer your question.

22. Madison asked some Grade 3 children about
their favourite school subject. The chart shows
her results.
a) How many children did Madison ask?
b) How many children prefer language arts?
How many do not?
c) Draw a bar graph to show Madison's data.
d) Write a question about Madison's data.
Answer your question.

Children's Favourite School Subjects

Subject	Number
ART	11
LANGUAGE ARTS	16
MATH	12
SCIENCE	5
SOCIAL STUDIES	9

8

23. These friends each bought stickers for
their collections.
How many stickers did each child buy?
a) Ali bought 4 strips of 5 stickers.
b) Kerri bought 3 strips of 4 stickers.
c) Tia bought 4 strips of 4 stickers.

24. What could the missing numbers be?
Find all the ways you can to solve each problem.
a) ___ × ___ = 12   b) ___ ÷ ___ = 3

Illustrated Glossary

Add: To combine 2 or more quantities to find how many altogether.

Addition fact: $3 + 4 = 7$ is an addition fact. The sum is 7. See also **Related facts**. The basic addition facts can be shown in an addition chart.

+	1	2	3	4	5	6	7	8	9
1	2	3	4	5	6	7	8	9	10
2	3	4	5	6	7	8	9	10	11
3	4	5	6	7	8	9	10	11	12
4	5	6	7	8	9	10	11	12	13
5	6	7	8	9	10	11	12	13	14
6	7	8	9	10	11	12	13	14	15
7	8	9	10	11	12	13	14	15	16
8	9	10	11	12	13	14	15	16	17
9	10	11	12	13	14	15	16	17	18

Addition sentence: An equation that shows an addition. $3 + 4 = 7$ is an addition sentence.

Array: A set of objects arranged in equal rows.

Attribute: A way to describe a shape or object; for example, number of sides, number of vertices.

Axis (plural: axes): A number line along the edge of a graph. We label each axis to tell what data it displays.

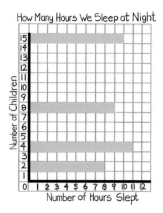

Bar graph: Shows data using bars on a grid. The graph below is a vertical bar graph. See **Axis** for an example of a horizontal bar graph.

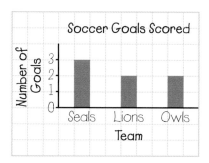

Base: The face that names an object. See **object**.

Base Ten Blocks: Blocks used to model whole numbers. Here is one way to model 158:

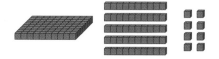

Calendar: An organized way to show days, weeks, months, and years. Usually, a calendar page shows one month.

Centimetre: A unit to measure length, width, and height. We write one centimetre as 1 cm.

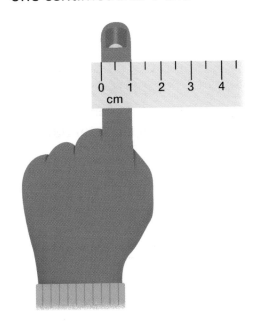

Chart: A way to organize numbers or information.

Animal Long Jumps

Animal	Distance
Snowshoe Hare	3 m
Red Kangaroo	5 m
Cougar	9 m
Northern Leopard Frog	1 m

Compare: 1. To look at how items are alike as well as different.
2. With numbers, to look at which is greater or less than the other. When we compare the numbers 5 and 8, we can write $5 < 8$ or $8 > 5$.

Cone: An object with a circular base, a curved surface, and a vertex.

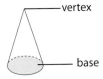

Core: The part of a pattern that repeats. See **Repeating pattern**.

Cube: An object with 6 faces that are all squares. Two faces meet at an edge.

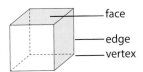

Cylinder: An object with 2 matching circular bases joined by a curved surface.

Data: Facts or information collected to learn about people or things.

Decreasing pattern: A pattern that grows smaller at each step.

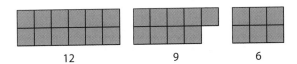

313

Denominator: The part of a fraction that tells how many equal parts are in one whole. The denominator is the bottom number in a fraction. Seven is the denominator in the example below.

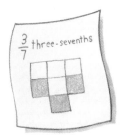

Diagonal: Means "on a slant."

Difference: The result of a subtraction. The difference of 9 and 5 is 4. We can write: $9 - 5 = 4$

Digit: See **Place value**.

Divide: To separate into equal parts or equal groups.

Divided by: In a division question like $16 \div 4$, we say that we are "dividing 16 by 4" when we create 4 equal groups out of 16 objects.

Division sentence: $6 \div 3 = 2$ is a division sentence. We say: 6 divided by 3 equals 2.

Doubles: The addition of 2 numbers that are the same. Doubles have an even sum.

Edge: When 2 surfaces of an object meet they form an edge. See also **Cube**.

Eighths: The fraction we get when we make 8 equal shares of an item. See also **Fractions**.

Equal groups: Groups that have the same number of things in each group. Equal groups can show a multiplication story.

These equal groups show that $3 \times 4 = 12$.

Equal parts: When we share, we can make equal parts. See also **Fractions**.

The pie is cut into 6 equal parts.

Equation: Uses the $=$ symbol to show 2 things that represent the same amount.
$5 + 2 = 7$ is an equation.
$5 + 2 = 3 + 4$ is an equation.
$3 + \square = 7$ is also an equation.

Estimate: 1. A thoughtful guess that is close to the answer, but not exact. **2.** To think about making a guess that is close but not exact.

Even number: Any number that you can reach when counting by 2s: 2, 4, 6, 8, 10, 12, 14, 16, 18, 20, 22, … . A counting number that ends in 0, 2, 4, 6, or 8 is an even number.

Face: Any flat surface on a three-dimensional object. This prism has all rectangular faces.

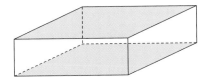

Fifths: The fraction we get when we make 5 equal shares of an item. See also **Fractions**.

Fourths: The fraction we get when we make 4 equal shares of an item. See also **Fractions**.

Fractions: Equal shares of an item are named with fractions. Some fractions are one-half $\left(\frac{1}{2}\right)$, one-third $\left(\frac{1}{3}\right)$, one-quarter or one-fourth $\left(\frac{1}{4}\right)$, one-fifth $\left(\frac{1}{5}\right)$, and one-tenth $\left(\frac{1}{10}\right)$.

Gram: A unit for measuring the mass of an object. We write one gram as 1 g.

Growing pattern: A pattern that grows larger at each step. May also be called **Increasing pattern**.

Half (plural: halves): The fraction we get when we make 2 equal shares of an item. See also **Fractions**.

Height: The measurement from top to bottom. See **Object**.

Hexagon: A polygon with 6 sides.

Hour: A unit for measuring time. There are sixty minutes in one hour. It might take about one hour to play a soccer game. We write one hour as 1 h.

Increasing pattern: A pattern that grows larger at each step.

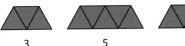
3   5   7

Kilogram: A unit for measuring the mass of an object. We write one kilogram as 1 kg.

Length: The measurement from end to end; how long something is. See **Shape**.

Line plot: A graph that uses an X to show each piece of data.

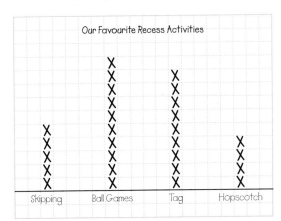

List: A way to organize numbers or information.

Favourite Recess Activities

Tag   Erin, Maya, Theo, Dave, Ange
Soccer   Pete, Anita, Keanna, Dee,
         Andrea, Soshana
Swings   Sandira
Slide   Mike, Poling

315

Mass: Measures how much matter is in an object. We measure mass in grams and kilograms.

Mental math: Calculating answers without using materials, or a calculator, or pencil and paper.

Metre: A unit for measuring length, width, and height. We write one metre as 1 m.

Minute: A unit for measuring time. It takes about one minute to button up a jacket. We write one minute as 1 min.

Multiplication fact: $3 \times 4 = 12$ is a multiplication fact. The chart shows some basic multiplication facts.

×	1	2	3	4	5
1	1	2	3	4	5
2	2	4	6	8	10
3	3	6	9	12	15
4	4	8	12	16	20
5	5	10	15	20	25

Multiplication sentence: $2 \times 3 = 6$ is a multiplication sentence. For $2 \times 3 = 6$, we say, 2 times 3 equals 6.

Multiply: Finding the total number in a set of equal groups or rows, or finding the total when adding the same number repeatedly.

Near doubles: The result of adding a number to the next counting number. For example, $7 + 8 = 15$.

Ninths: The fraction we get when we make 9 equal shares of an item. See also **Fraction**.

Number line: A line with evenly spaced numbers marked in order.

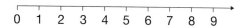

Numerator: The part of a fraction that tells how many equal parts to count. The numerator is the top number in a fraction. Three is the numerator in the fraction below.

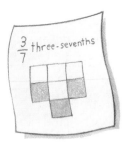

Object: Has length, width, and height. When we work with objects we can look for faces, edges, vertices, and bases. We name some objects by the number and shape of the bases.

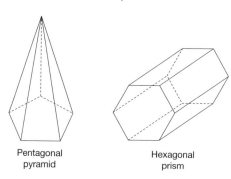

Pentagonal pyramid　　　　Hexagonal prism

Octagon: A polygon with 8 sides.

Odd number: Any number that you would never reach when counting by 2s: 1, 3, 5, 7, 9, 11, 13, 15, 17, 19, 21, 23, 25, … .
A counting number that ends in 1, 3, 5, 7, or 9 is an odd number.

Operation: Addition, subtraction, multiplication, and division are all operations.

Order: To place numbers in sequence according to some rule.

Pattern rule: Tells about a pattern or tells how to make a pattern.
1, 4, 7, 10, 13, 16, …
The pattern rule for this pattern is: Start at 1. Add 3 each time.

Pentagon: A polygon with 5 sides.

Perimeter: The distance around a shape. We can find perimeter by measuring and adding side lengths. The perimeter of this rectangle is:
2 cm + 4 cm + 2 cm + 4 cm = 12 cm

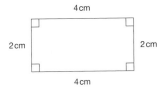

Pictograph: Uses pictures or symbols to show data.

Unusual Animals Seen in a Year	
Ostriches	★ ★ ★
Alpacas	★ ★ ★ ★ ★ ★ ★ ★ ★ ★
Bison	★ ★ ★ ★ ★ ★ ★
Llamas	★ ★ ★ ★ ★ ★ ★ ★

Place value: The value of a digit that appears in a number. The value of each digit in a number depends on its place in the number.

Hundreds	Tens	Ones
4	9	7

The value of this digit is 4 hundreds, or 400.
The value of this digit is 9 tens, or 90.
The value of this digit is 7 ones, or 7.

We write: 497
We say: four hundred ninety-seven

Polygon: A closed shape made up of 3 or more straight sides. We name a polygon by the number of its sides. For example, a 5-sided polygon is a pentagon.

Prism: An object with 2 bases that match. The shape of the bases gives the name to the prism.

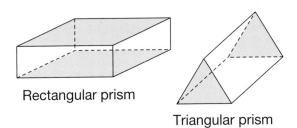

Rectangular prism

Triangular prism

Product: The result of multiplying numbers together. In the multiplication sentence below, 6 is the product.
2 × 3 = 6

Pyramid: An object with 1 base and triangular faces that meet at a point. The shape of the base gives the name to the pyramid.

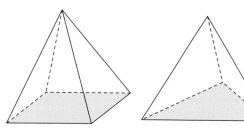

Rectangular pyramid   Triangular pyramid

Quadrilateral: A polygon with 4 sides.

Quarters: 1. The fraction we get when we make 4 equal shares of an item. **2.** The coin for 25 cents.

Rectangle: A quadrilateral with pairs of equal sides opposite to each other, and shaped with square corners.

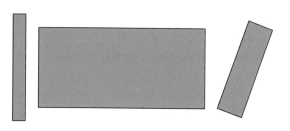

Referent: Something you can think about to help you estimate a measurement, or a count. Your finger width is a referent for 1 cm. Having 10 counters in your hand can be a referent for estimating the number of counters on your desk.

Related facts: Facts that use the same numbers, but may use different operations. Addition and subtraction have related facts.
$4 + 3 = 7, 3 + 4 = 7$,
$7 - 3 = 4$, and $7 - 4 = 3$,
are all related facts.
Multiplication and division have related facts.
$5 \times 2 = 10, 2 \times 5 = 10$,
$10 \div 5 = 2$, and $10 \div 2 = 5$,
are all related facts.

Repeating pattern: A pattern with a core that repeats. The smallest part that repeats is the core.

core

Scale: The numbers written along either axis in a graph.
The number of items each unit on a bar graph represents.

Second: A unit for measuring time. It takes about one second to blink your eyes. There are sixty seconds in one minute. We write one second as 1 s.

Sevenths: The fraction we get when we make 7 equal shares of an item. See also **Fractions**.

Shape: A geometric figure or its diagram.

Circle   Square   Triangle   Rectangle

Shrinking pattern: A pattern that grows smaller at each step. May also be called **Decreasing pattern**.

Sixths: The fraction we get when we make 6 equal shares of an item. See **Fractions**.

Skeleton: The frame of an object that shows its edges and vertices.

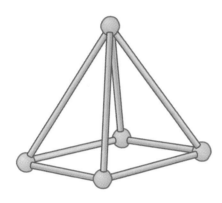

Skip count: To count following a pattern. For example, skip counting by 2s:
2, 4, 6, 8, 10, 12, 14, 16, …
Skip counting by 5s:
5, 10, 15, 20, 25, 30, 35, 40, …

Sorting rule: Names the attribute or attributes used to decide if an item belongs in a group. In this example, the sorting rule is "polygons with 5 sides and polygons with 3 sides."

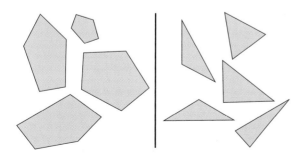

Sphere: An object shaped like a ball.

Square: A polygon with 4 equal sides and where every corner is a square corner.

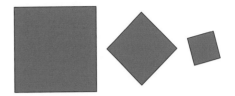

Standard form: Numbers written using digits: for example, 37 or 904.

Subtract: To remove one quantity from another to find how many are left, or, to find the missing part in a combination problem.

Subtraction fact: $11 - 7 = 4$ and $11 - 4 = 7$ are subtraction facts. See also **Related facts**.

Sum: The result of an addition. The sum of 2 and 3 is 5, since $2 + 3 = 5$.

Tally chart: A chart on which a count is kept.

Black	ℍℍ ℍℍ
Red	ℍℍ ℍℍ
Orange	ℍℍ ℍℍ
Green	ℍℍ ℍℍ

Tally mark: A way of counting items by making one mark for each item you count, and grouping by 5s as you go. See **Tally chart** for an example of tally marks.

Tenths: The fraction we get when we make 10 equal shares of an item. See also **Fractions**.

Thirds: The fraction we get when we make 3 equal shares of an item. See also **Fractions**.

Thousand: The number we get by combining 10 groups of 100.

Times: The multiplication sentence 3 × 4 = 12 can be read as "3 times 4 is equal to 12."

Title: The part of a graph that tells what the graph is about.

Triangle: A polygon with 3 sides.

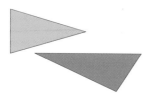

Unit: A standard amount used for measuring.

Vertex (plural: vertices): 1. A point where 2 sides of a shape meet. **2.** A point where 3 or more edges of an object meet. **3.** On a cone, the highest point above the base.

Width: The distance across something; how wide it is. See **Shape**.

Index

Acknowledgments

Pearson Education would like to thank the Royal Canadian Mint for the illustrative use of Canadian coins in this textbook. In addition, the publisher wishes to thank the following sources for photographs, illustrations, and other materials used in this book. Care has been taken to determine and locate ownership of copyright material in this text. We will gladly receive information enabling us to rectify any errors or omissions in credits.

Photography

Cover: David Nunuk/firstlight.ca; p. 2 Ian Crysler; p. 3 Ian Crysler; p. 6 Ian Crysler; p. 10 Galen Rowell/Corbis/Magma Photo; p. 18 Ian Crysler; p. 20 Ian Crysler; p. 22 Ian Crysler; p. 24 Ian Crysler; p. 29 Ian Crysler; p. 35 Ian Crysler; p. 38 Ian Crysler; p. 41 Ray Boudreau; p. 50 Ian Crysler; p. 54 Ian Crysler; p. 56 Ian Crysler; p. 57 Ian Crysler; p. 58 (top right) Arlene Jean Gee/ShutterStock; p. 58 (top left) Steven J. Kazlowski/Alamy; p. 58 (bottom) Ian Crysler; p. 62 Ian Crysler; p. 68 Ian Crysler; p. 71 Ray Boudreau; p. 72 (top) Keith Levit/ShutterStock; p. 72 (bottom) Ian Crysler; p. 73 Ian Crysler; p. 74 Photodisc Collection/Photodisc Blue; p. 75 Ian Crysler; p. 79 Gunter Marx/Alamy; pp. 80-81 Natalia Bratslavsky/ShutterStock; p. 81 (inset left) Peter Carroll/Alamy; p. 81 (inset right) Tom Mackie/Alamy; p. 89 Ian Crysler; p. 90 Ian Crysler; p. 92 pmphoto/ShutterStock; p. 94 JUPITERIMAGES/Creatas/Alamy; p. 95 Terry Renna/Associated Press; p. 100 Ian Crysler; p. 101 Ian Crysler; p. 104 Ian Crysler; p. 106 Ian Crysler; p. 107 Calaway Park/Bruce Edwards Photography; p. 108 Courtesy of Jim Hawkings; p. 109 (centre) Calaway Park/Bruce Edwards Photography; p. 109 (bottom) Ray Boudreau; p. 110 Alaska Stock LLC/Alamy; p. 115 Corel Collection; p. 116 Ian Crysler; p. 117 Ian Crysler; p. 118 Ian Crysler; p. 120 Courtesy of the Times Colonist; p. 123 (top) The Canadian Press/Rene Johnston; p. 123 (bottom) ShutterStock; p. 128 Chris Cheadle/Alamy; p. 129 Konrad Zelazowski/Alamy; p. 134 Ian Crysler; p. 136 Ian Crysler; p. 138 (top left) Daniel Pangbourne/Digital Vision/Getty Images; p. 138 (top centre) Corel; p. 138 (top right) AJA Productions/Stone/Getty Images; p. 138 (bottom) Ian Crysler; p. 139 Ian Crysler; p. 140 Ulana Switucha/Alamy; p. 143 Iztok Noc/ShutterStock; p. 145 Ian Crysler; p. 146 Ian Crysler; p. 149 Ian Crysler; p. 152 Ray Boudreau; p. 153 Ian Crysler; p. 154 Ian Crysler; p. 155 Ian Crysler; p. 157 Ian Crysler; p. 160 (top) Ray Boudreau; p. 160 (bottom) Ian Crylser; p. 161 Ian Crysler; p. 162 Ian Crysler; p. 163 Ian Crysler; p. 164 Ian Crysler; p. 165 Ian Crysler; p. 167 Ian Crysler; p. 169 Ian Crysler; p. 171 Ian Crysler; p. 178 Ian Crysler; p. 179 Ian Crysler; p. 182 Ian Crysler; p. 185 Ray Boudreau; p. 188 Ray Boudreau; p. 189 Ray Boudreau; p. 190 Ray Boudreau; p. 192 Ian Crysler; p. 196 Ian Crysler; p. 197 Ian Crysler; p. 200 Ian Crysler; p. 211 Ian Crysler; p. 216 Ken McLaren; p. 218 (top left) Raine Vara/Alamy; p. 218 (top right) Allan Freed/ShutterStock; p. 218 (bottom) Ian Crysler; p. 220 Richard Garner/Canadian Museum of Civilization/Artifact VII-c-106a, b; Image S94-6803; p. 222 Ian Crysler; p. 225 Ian Crysler; p. 228 Ian Crysler; p. 229 (top) Photodisc Green/David Buffington; p. 229 (bottom) Ian Crysler; pp. 238-239 Image Source Pink/Alamy; p. 239 (top) Photo courtesy of the Western College of Veterinary Medicine, University of Saskatchewan (www.wcvm.com); p. 239 (bottom) Judy Tejero/ShutterStock; p. 240 Ian Crysler; p. 247 Ray Boudreau; p. 248 (left) Serg Zastavkin/ShutterStock; p. 248 (centre) Brian Durell/maXx Images; p. 248 (right) John W. Wall/Alamy; p. 249 (left & right) Photos.com/Jupiterimages Unlimited; p. 252 Ian Crysler; p. 254 The Canadian Press/Richard Lam; p. 256 Don Smetzer/Stone/Getty Images; p. 259 Ian Crysler; p. 264 Photo courtesy of the Western College of Veterinary Medicine, University of Saskatchewan (www.wcvm.com); p. 265 Photo courtesy of the Western College of Veterinary Medicine, University of Saskatchewan (www.wcvm.com); p. 268 Ian Crysler; p. 271 Ray Boudreau; p. 272 Ian Crysler; p. 273 Ian Crysler; p. 276 Ian Crysler; p. 283 Ian Crysler; p. 284 Ian Crysler; p. 287 Ian Crysler; p. 290 Ian Crysler; p. 291 Ian Crysler; p. 293 Ulrike Hammerich/ShutterStock; p. 299 Zuzule/ShutterStock; p. 306 Ian Crysler; p. 307 Ian Crysler

Illustrations

Amid Studios, Steve Attoe, Christiane Beauregard, Jackie Besteman, Doris Barrette, Kasia Charko, François Escalmel, Philippe Germain, Linda Hendry, Brian Hughes, André Labrie, Steve MacEachern, Tad Majewski, Dave Mazierski, Paul McCusker, Allan Moon, Mike Opsahl, Dusan Petriçic, Michel Rabagliati, Scott Ritchie, Bill Slavin, Neil Stewart/NSV Productions, Craig Terlson, Carl Wiens